Owner Name ______________________________

Phone Number ____________________________

Email Address ____________________________

Reward if found and returned is $______________

Copyright Notice

Business Performance Advisors LLC

c/o Law Office of Michael E. Young PLLC

5960 W. Parker Rd., Ste. 278 PMB 421

Plano, Texas 75093 USA

First Edition, February 2014

Published by Business Performance Advisors LLC.

Instructions

The ClockMap™ Daily Planner is a nonlinear planner that makes it easy to schedule your tasks, meetings, and other events in your work and personal life.

When you turn this page, you will notice two analog clock faces: the left page is where you schedule your morning (the "AM" clock face); and the right page is for your afternoon and evening activities (the "PM" clock face).

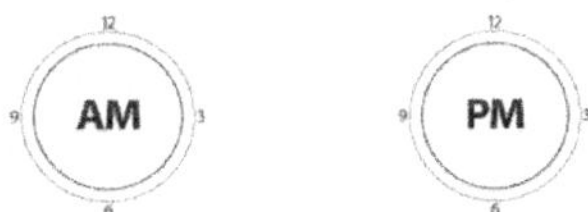

This daily planning method is very simple to use. For example, if you're having lunch with your friend at 1 p.m., simply draw a line (a spoke) from the edge of the 1 p.m. location on the "PM" clock face and write your lunch appointment at the end of the spoke.

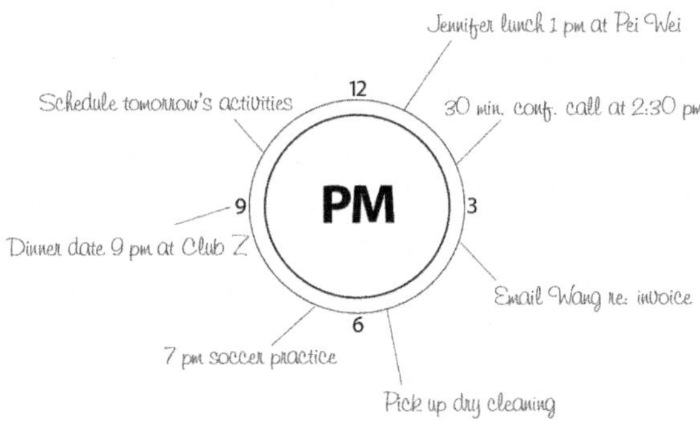

For more information, visit our website at **ClockMapDailyPlanner.com**

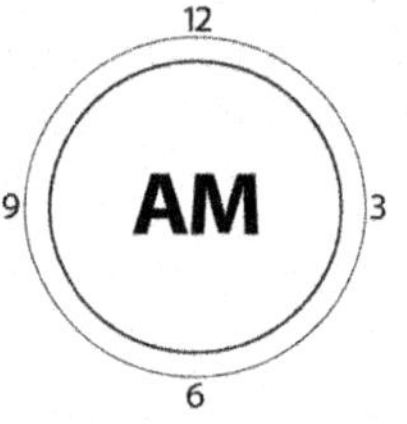
12
9
AM
3
6

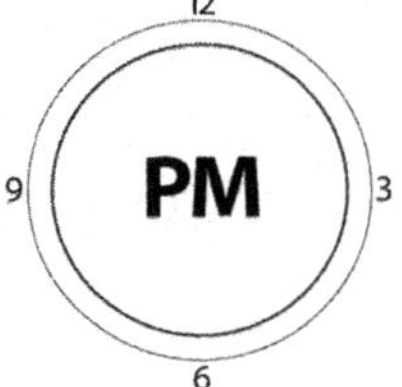
12
9
PM
3
6

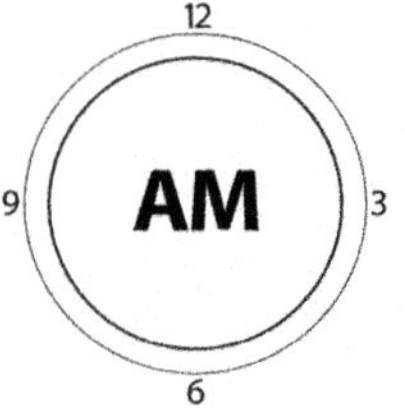
12
9
AM
3
6

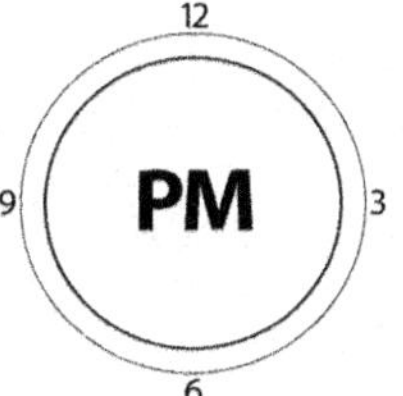
12
9
PM
3
6

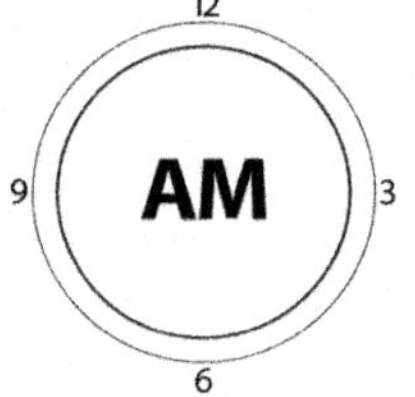
12
9
AM
3
6

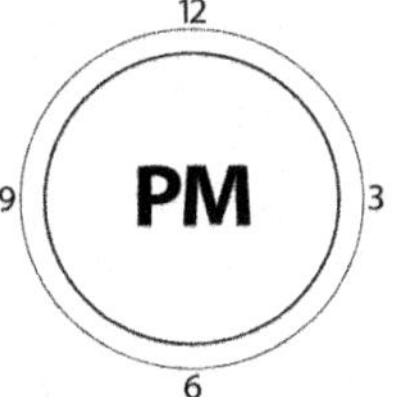
12
9
PM
3
6

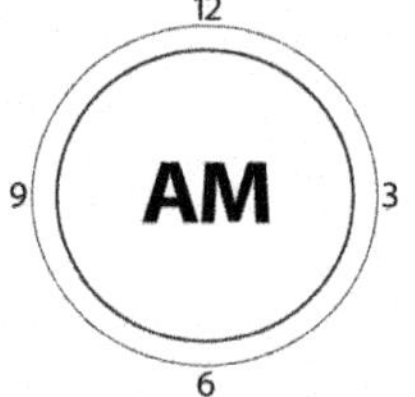
12
9
AM
3
6

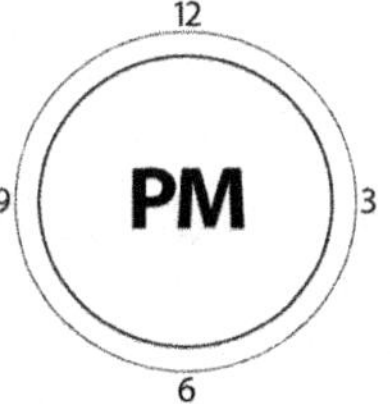
12
9
PM
3
6

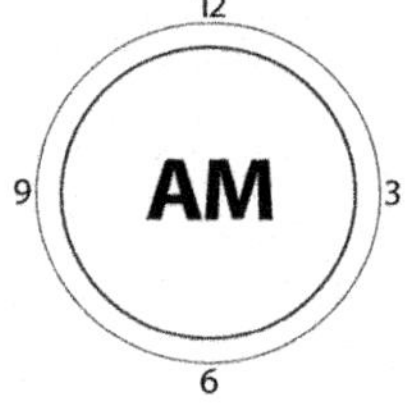
12
9
AM
3
6

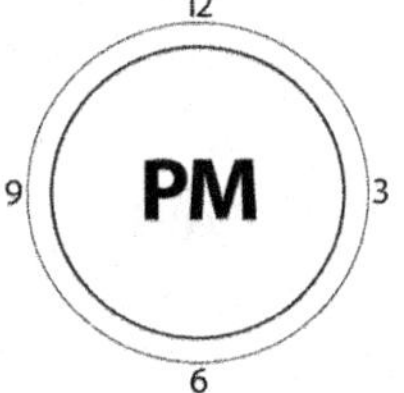
12
9
PM
3
6

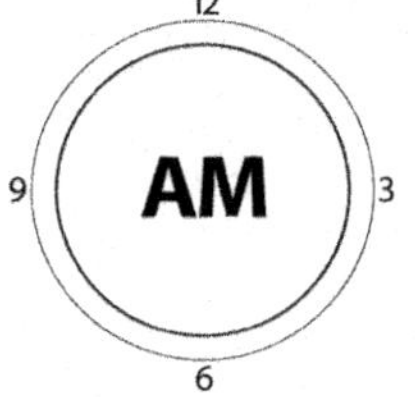
12
9
AM
3
6

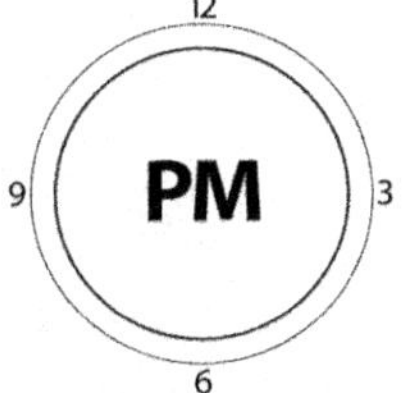
12
9
PM
3
6

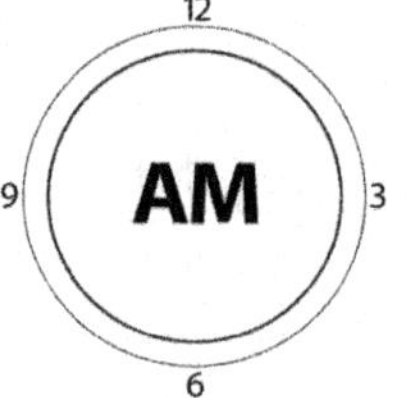
12
9
AM
3
6

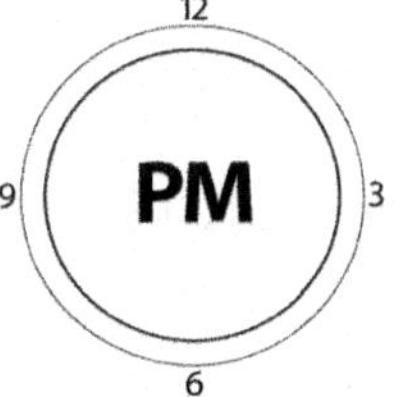
12
9
PM
3
6

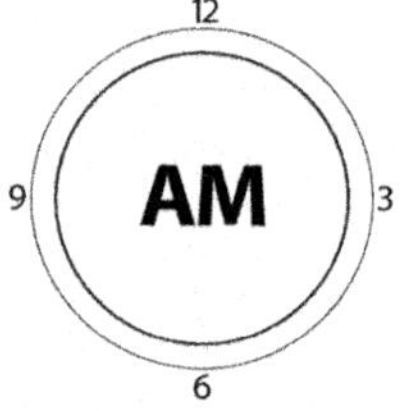
12
9
AM
3
6

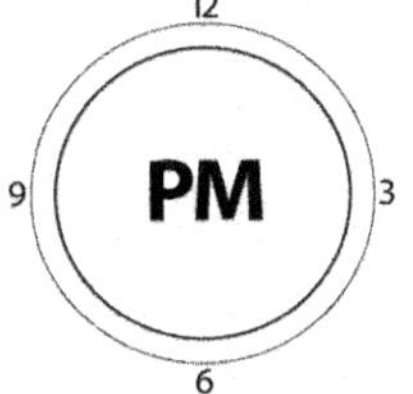
12
9
PM
3
6

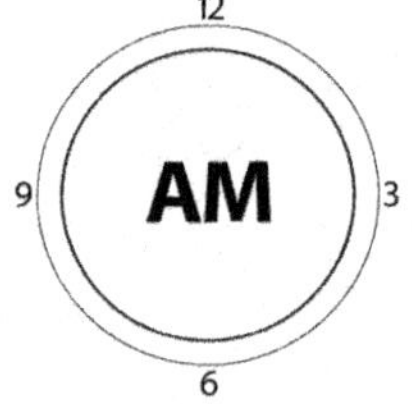
12
9
AM
3
6

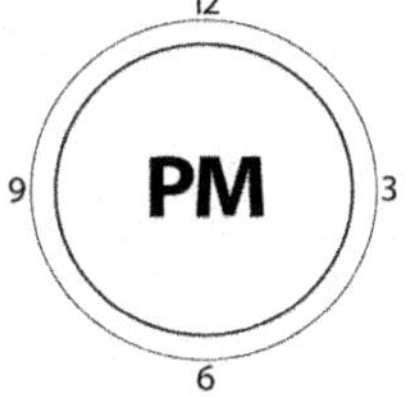
12
9
PM
3
6

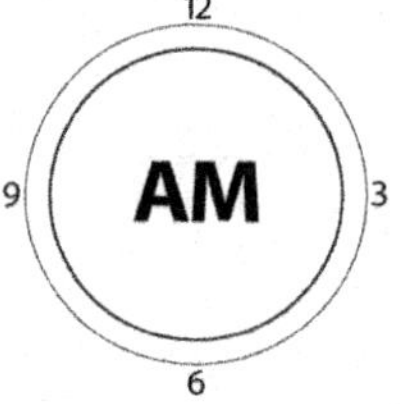
12
9
AM
3
6

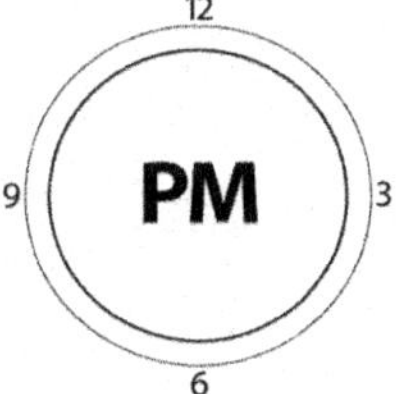
12
9
PM
3
6

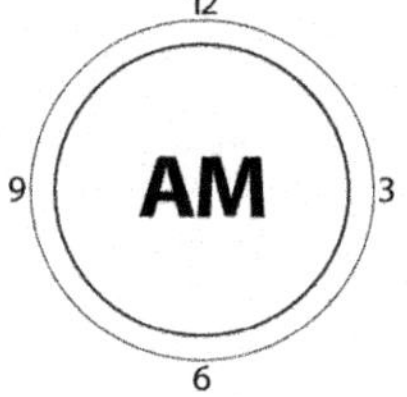
12
9
AM
3
6

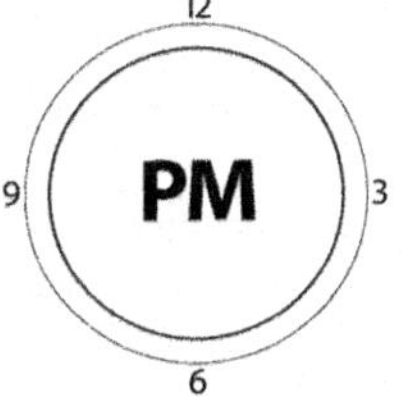
12
9
PM
3
6

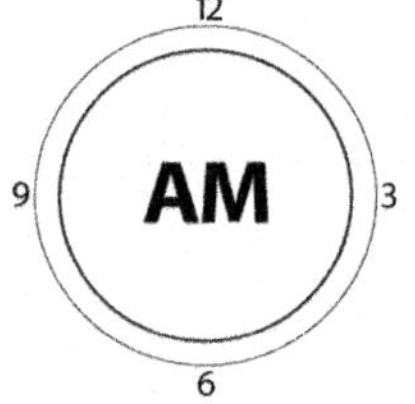
12
9
AM
3
6

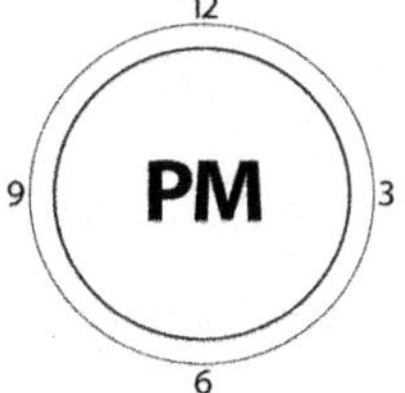
12
9
PM
3
6

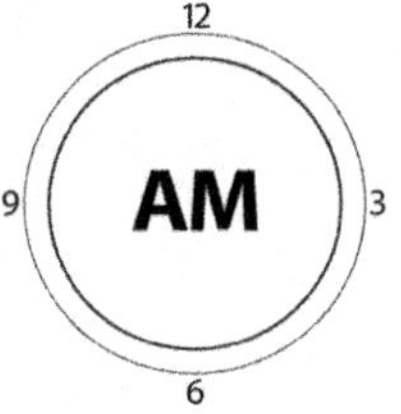
12
9
AM
3
6

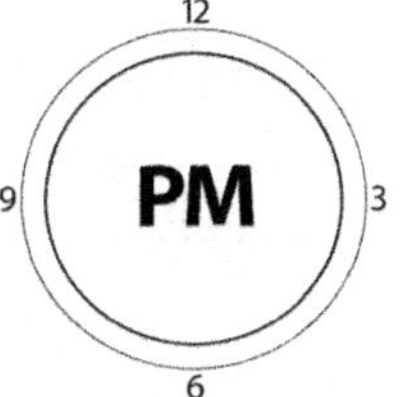
12
9
PM
3
6

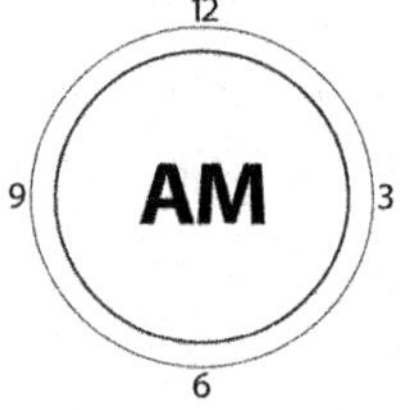
12
9
AM
3
6

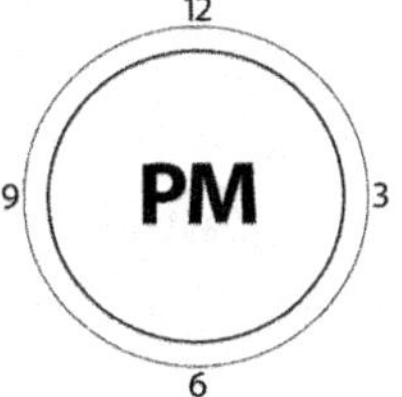
12
9
PM
3
6

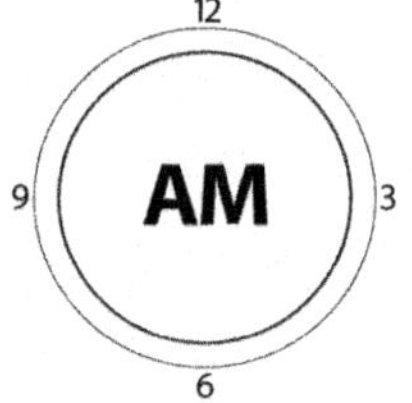
12
9
AM
3
6

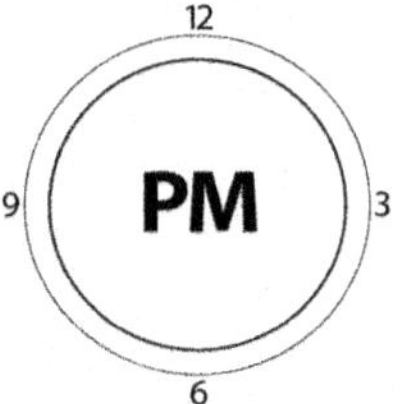
12
9
PM
3
6

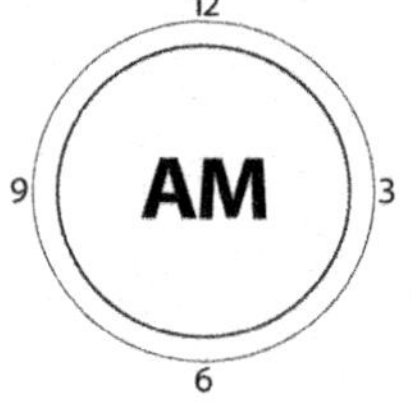
12
9
AM
3
6

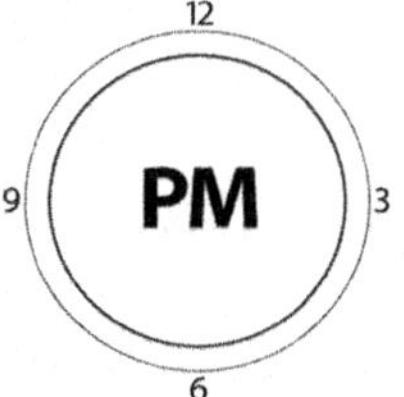
12
9
PM
3
6

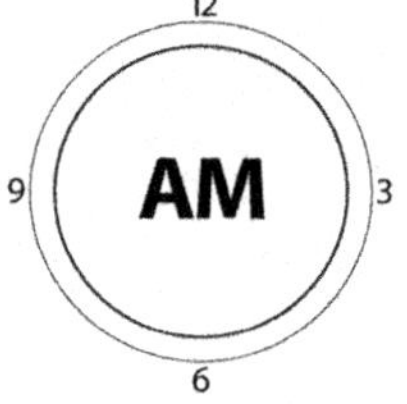
12
9
AM
3
6

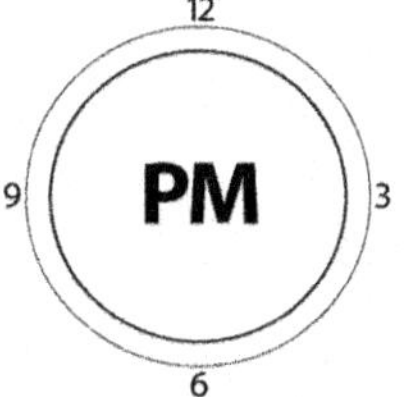
12
9
PM
3
6

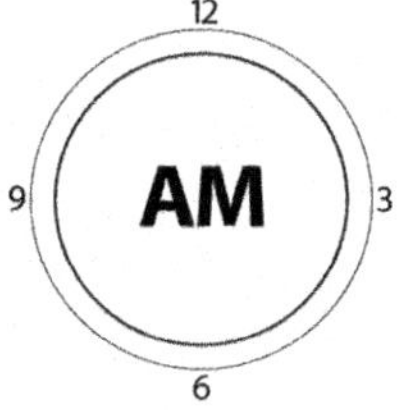
12
9
AM
3
6

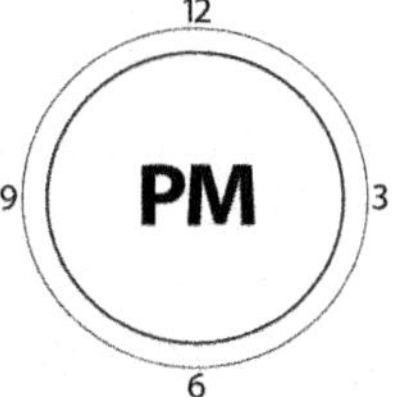
12
9
PM
3
6

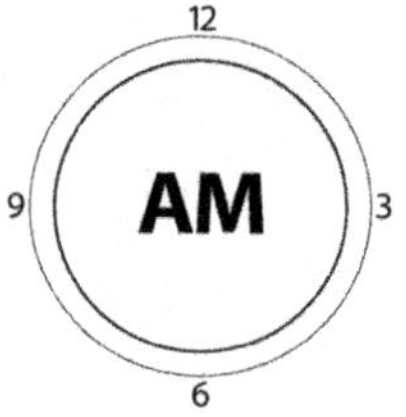
12
9
AM
3
6

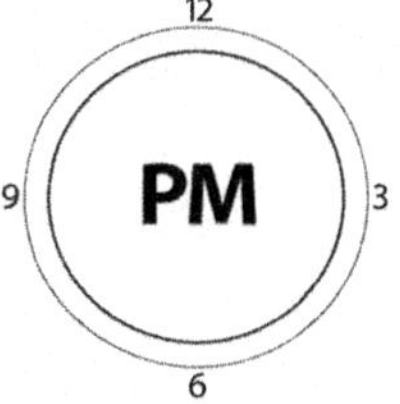
12
9
PM
3
6

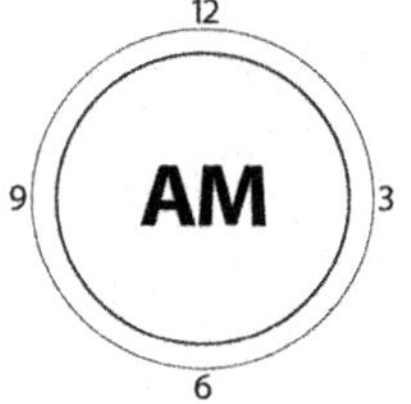
12
9
AM
3
6

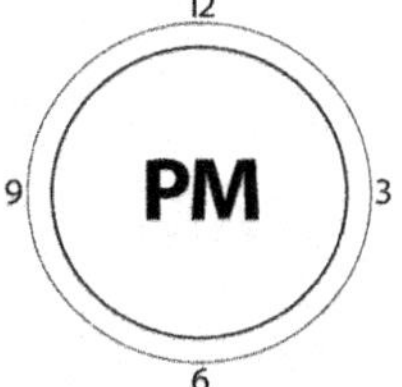
12
9
PM
3
6

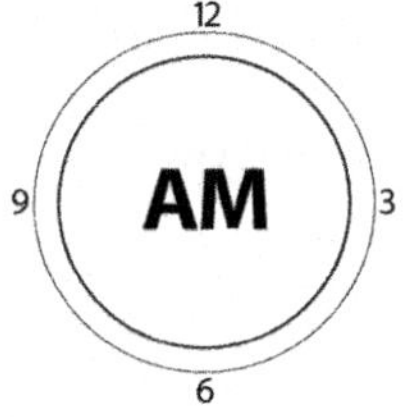
12
9
AM
3
6

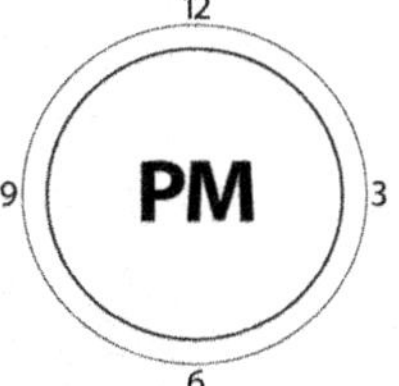
12
9
PM
3
6

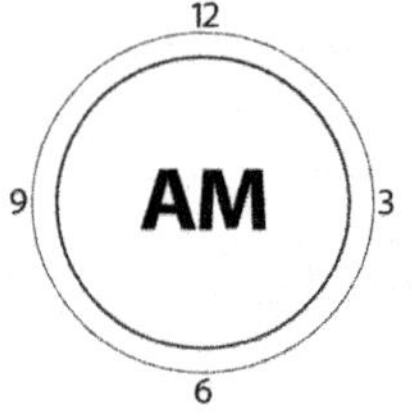
12
9
AM
3
6

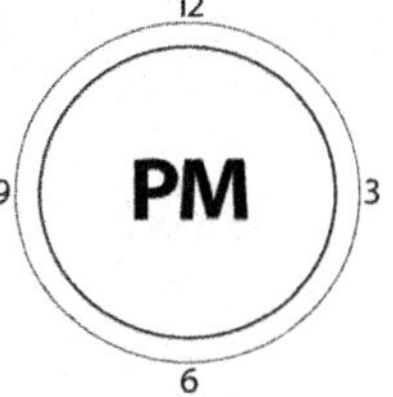
12
9
PM
3
6

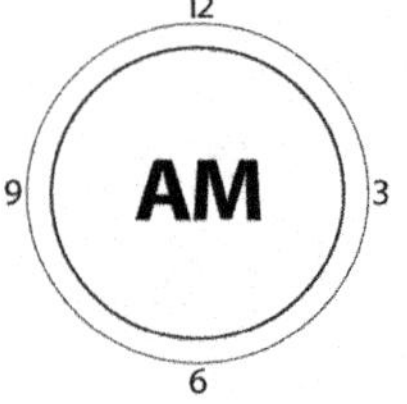
12
9
AM
3
6

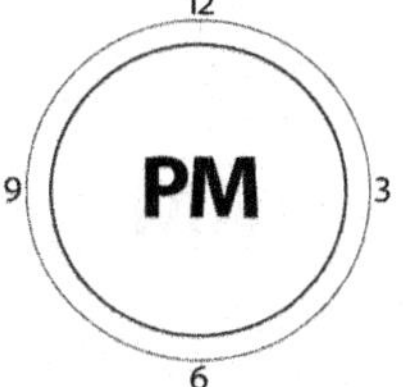
12
9
PM
3
6

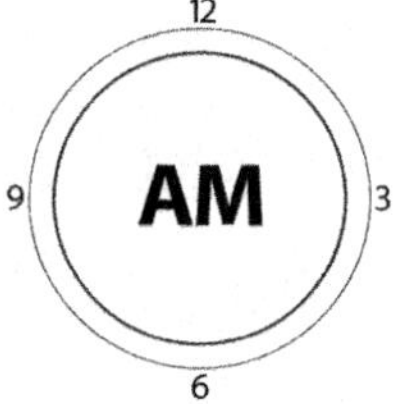
12
9
AM
3
6

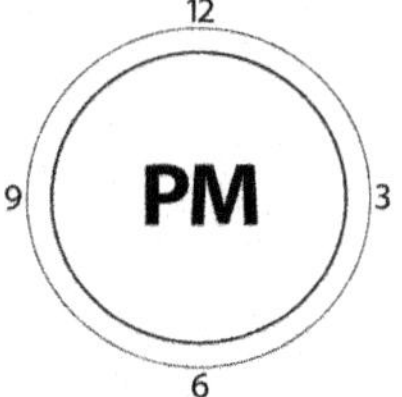
12
9
PM
3
6

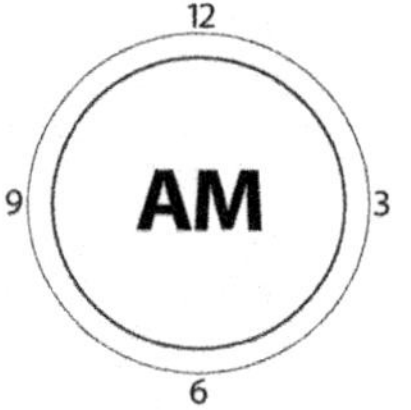
12
9
AM
3
6

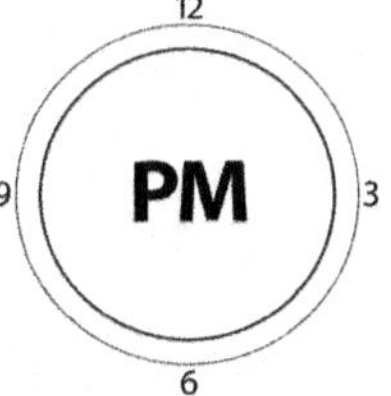
12
9
PM
3
6

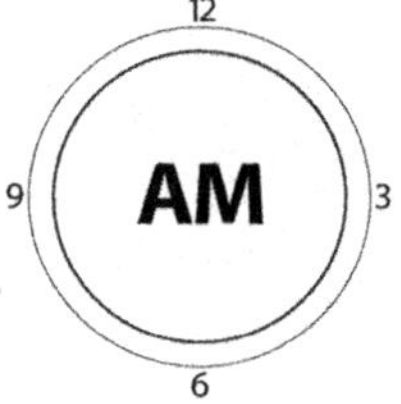
12
9
AM
3
6

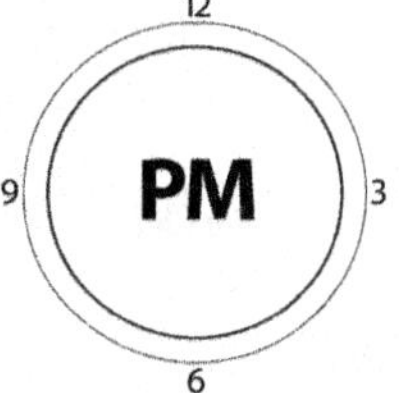
12
9
PM
3
6

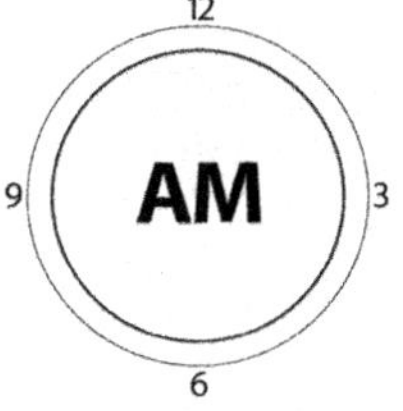
12
9
AM
3
6

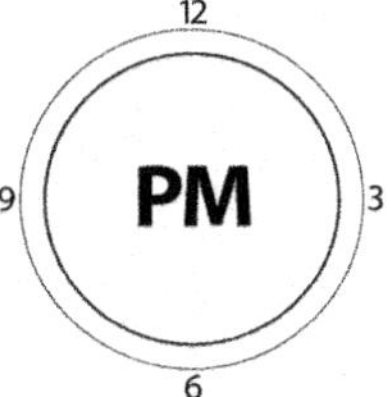
12
9
PM
3
6

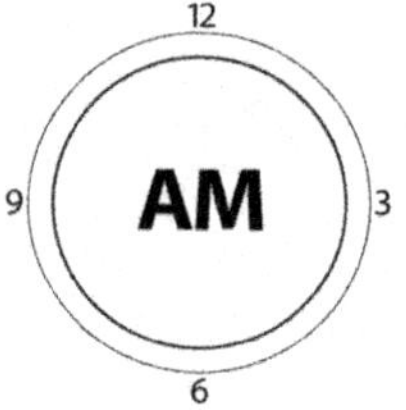
12
9
AM
3
6

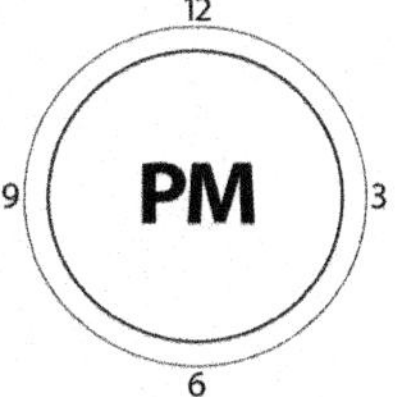
12
9
PM
3
6

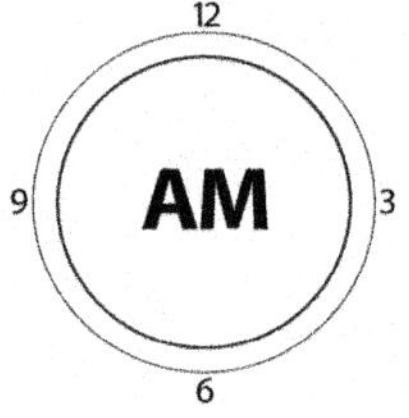
12
9
AM
3
6

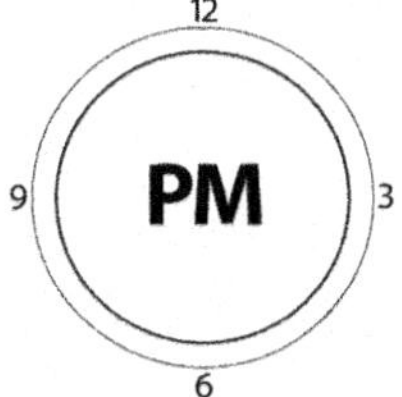
12
9
PM
3
6

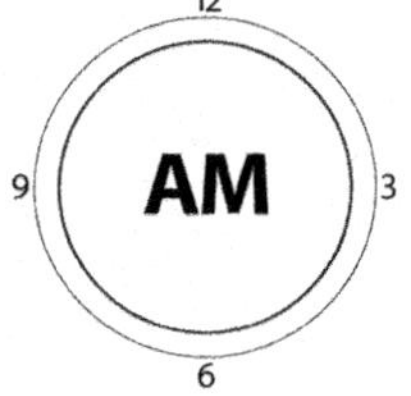
12
9
AM
3
6

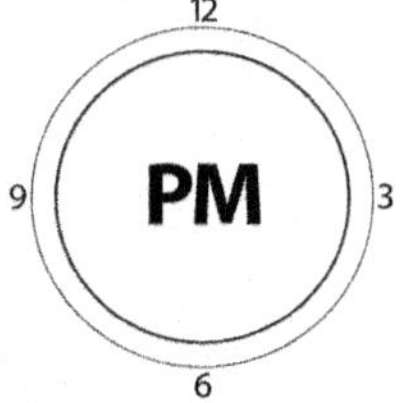
12
9
PM
3
6

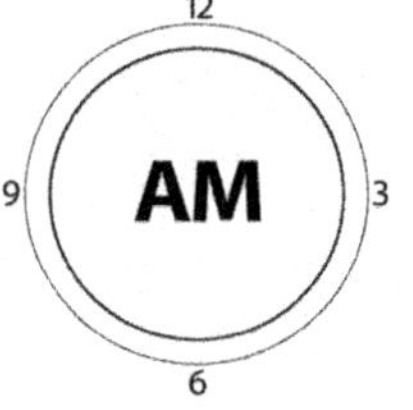
12
9
AM
3
6

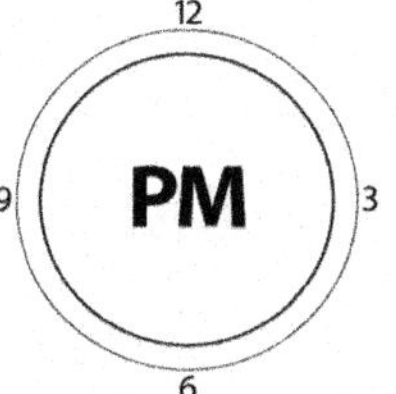
12
9
PM
3
6

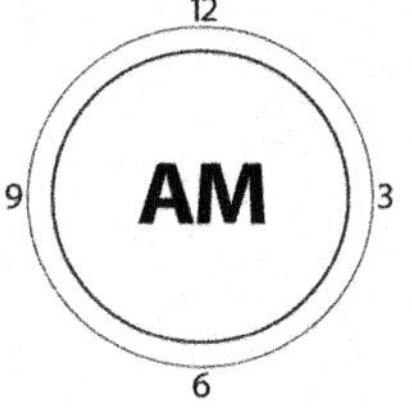
12
9
AM
3
6

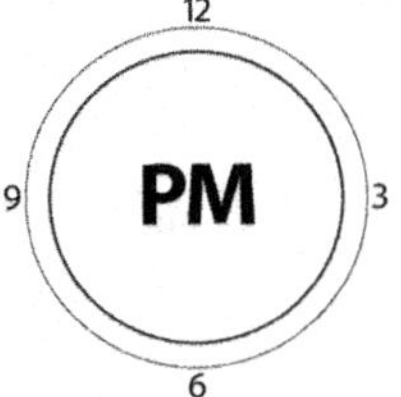
12
9
PM
3
6

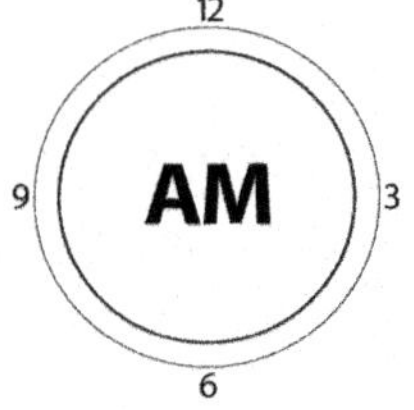
12
9
AM
3
6

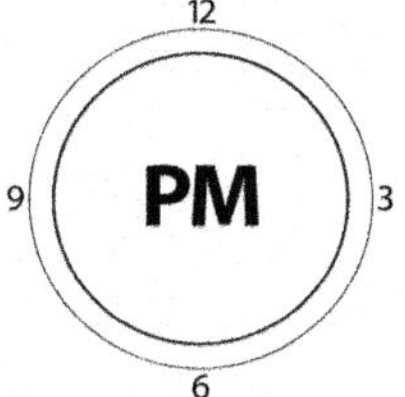
12
9
PM
3
6

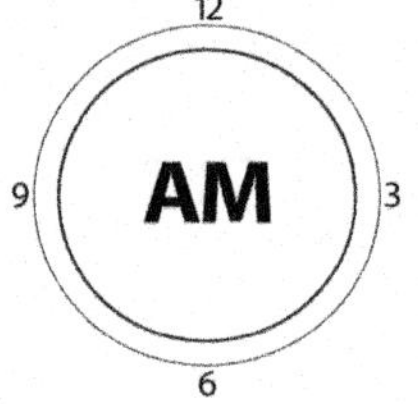
12
9
AM
3
6

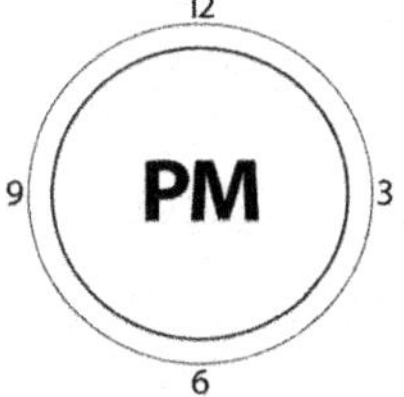
12
9
PM
3
6

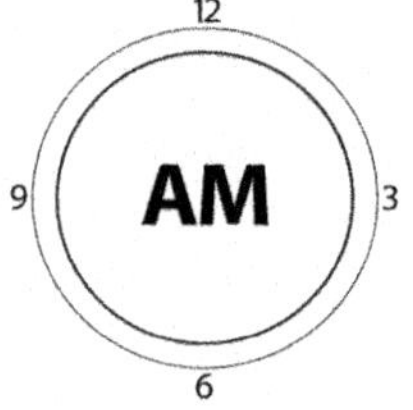
12
9
AM
3
6

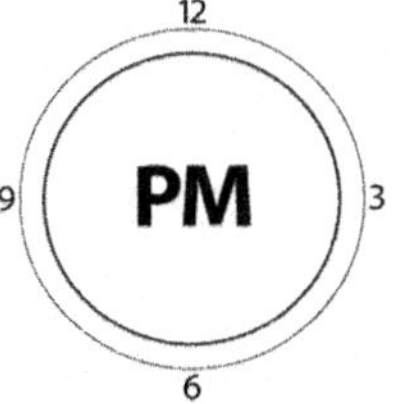
12
9
PM
3
6

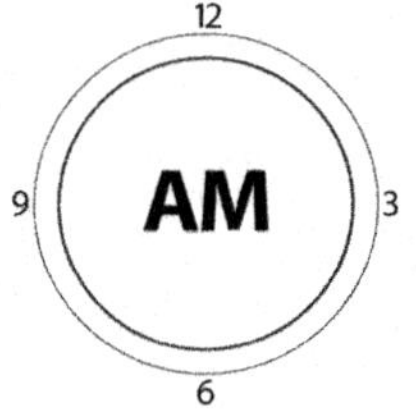
12
9
AM
3
6

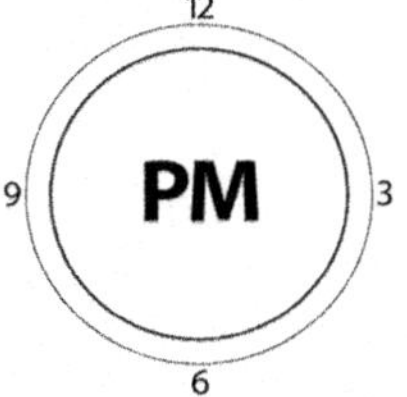
12
9
PM
3
6

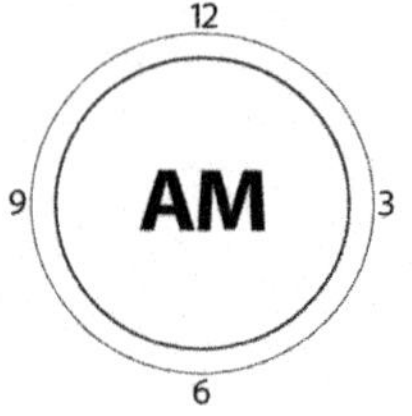
12
9
AM
3
6

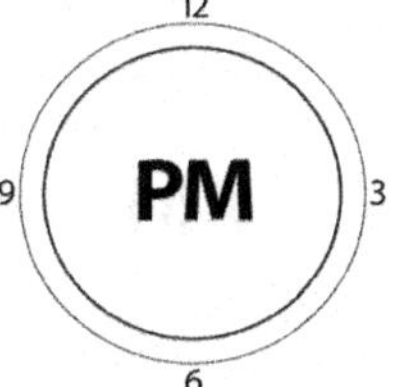
12
9
PM
3
6

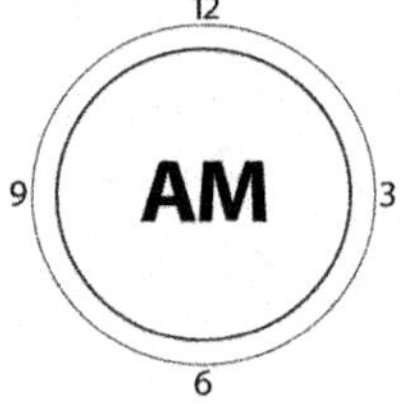
12
9
AM
3
6

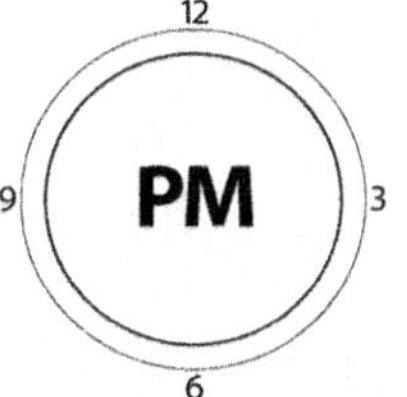
12
9
PM
3
6

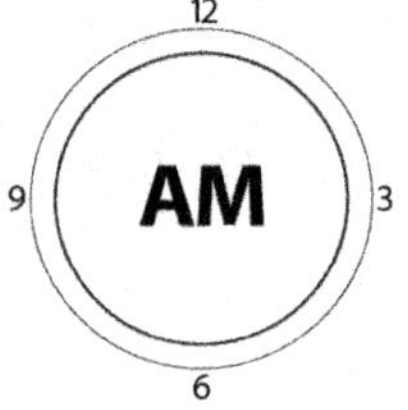
12
9
AM
3
6

12
9
PM
3
6

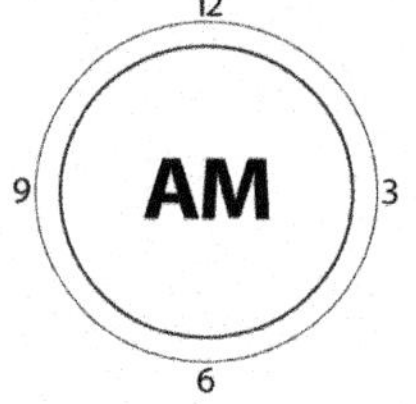
12
9
AM
3
6

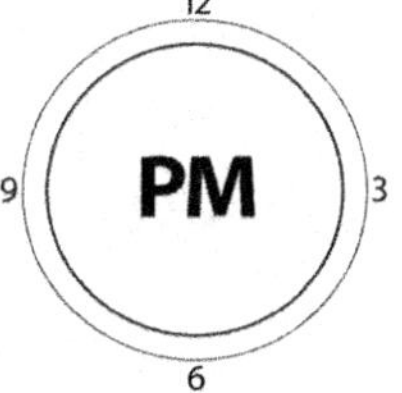
12
9
PM
3
6

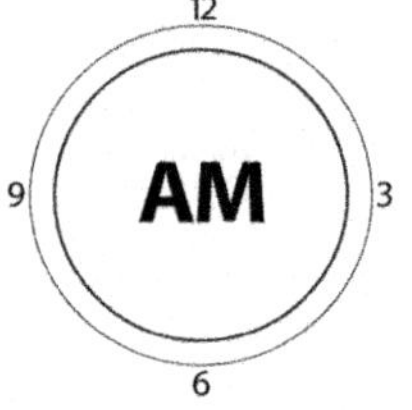
12
9
AM
3
6

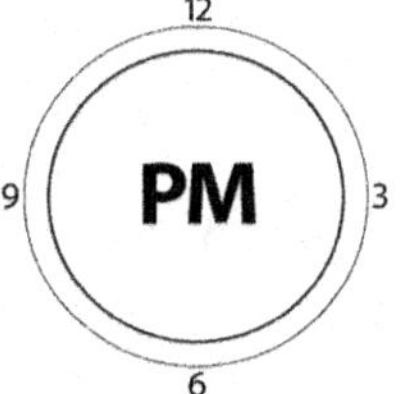
12
9
PM
3
6

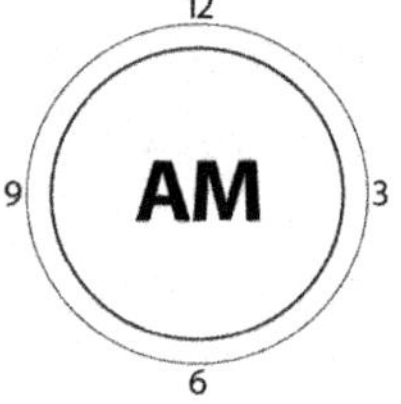
12
9
AM
3
6

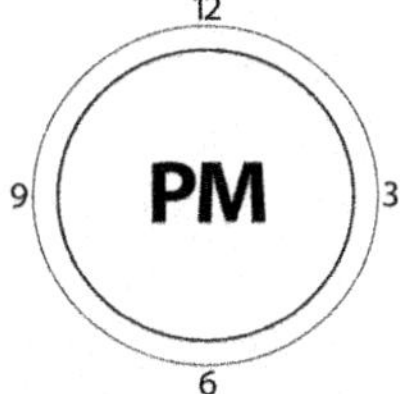
12
9
PM
3
6

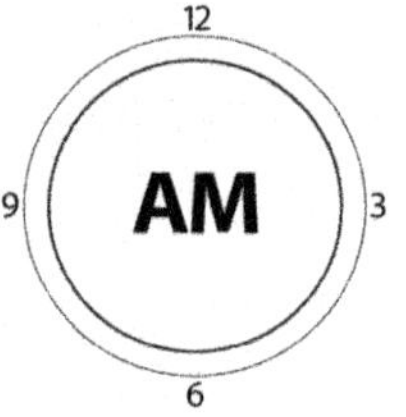
12
9
AM
3
6

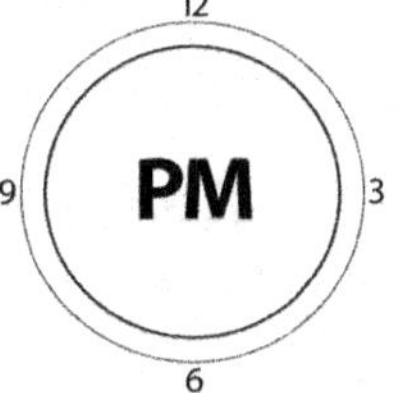
12
9
PM
3
6

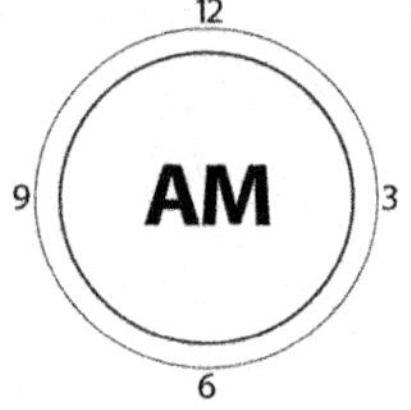
12
9
AM
3
6

12
9
PM
3
6

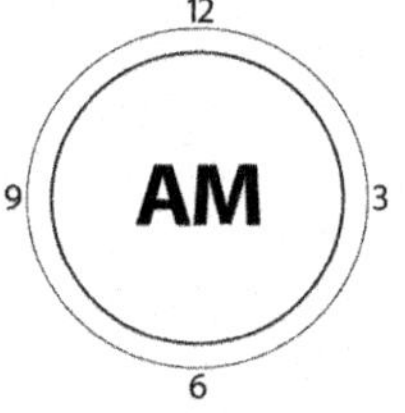
12
9
AM
3
6

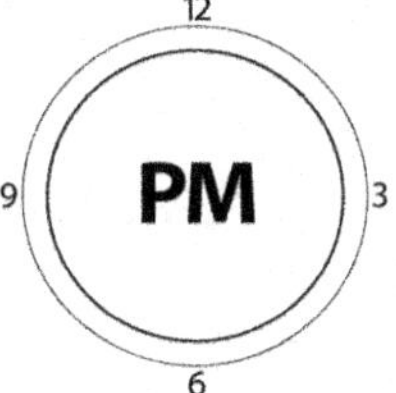
12
9
PM
3
6

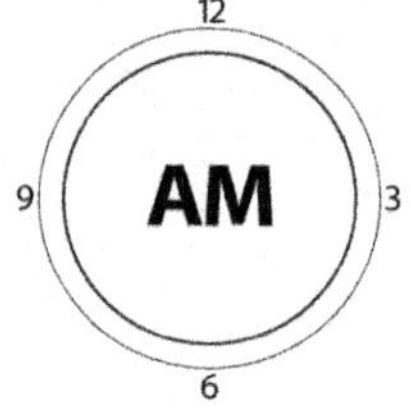
12
9
AM
3
6

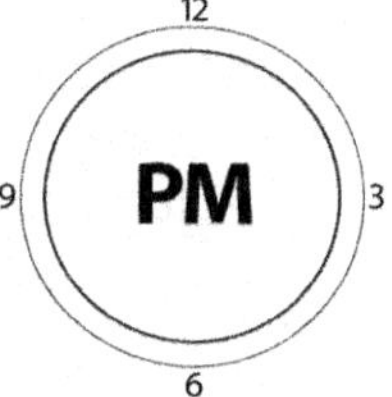
12
9
PM
3
6

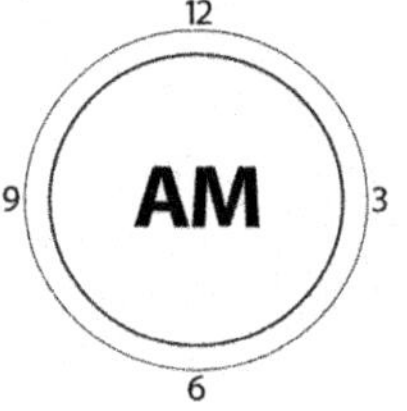
12
9
AM
3
6

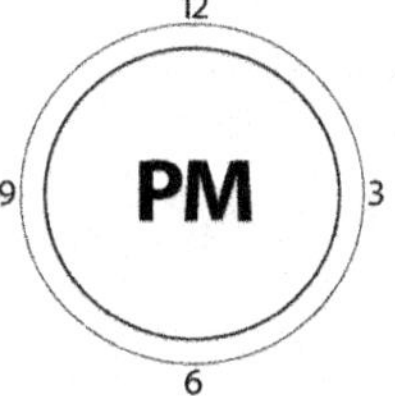
12
9
PM
3
6

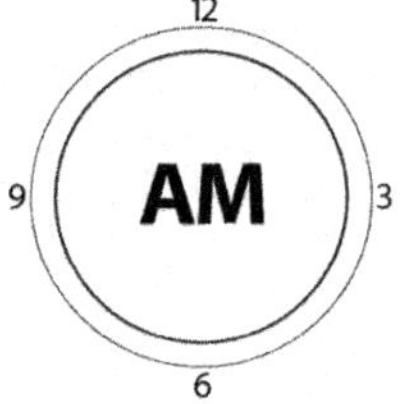
12
9
AM
3
6

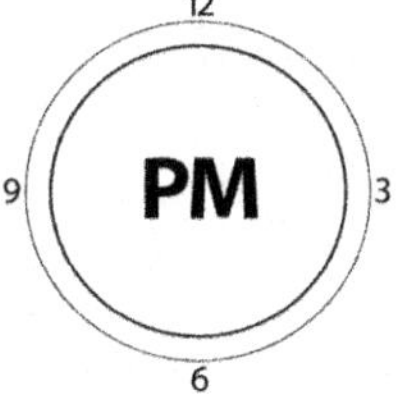
12
9
PM
3
6

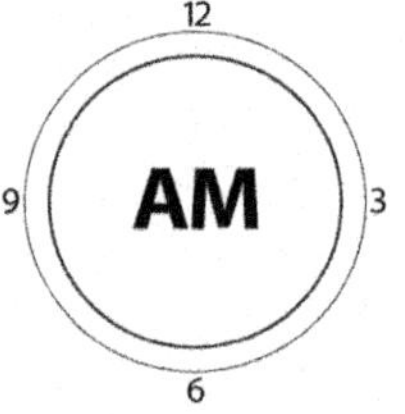
12
9
AM
3
6

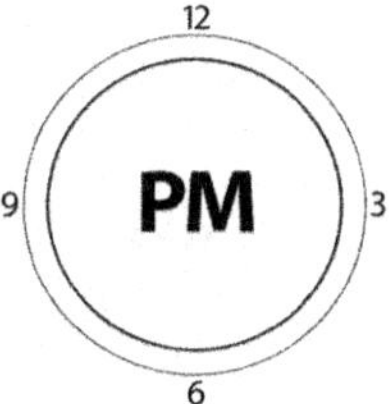
12
9
PM
3
6

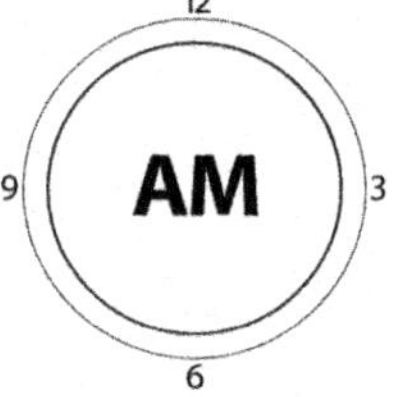
12
9
AM
3
6

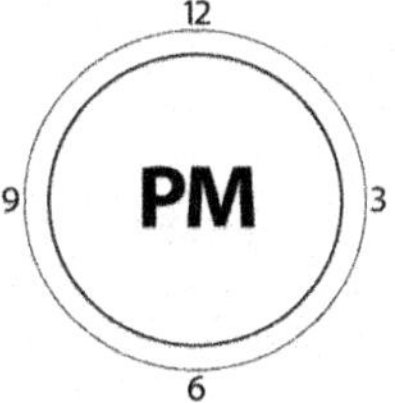
12
9
PM
3
6

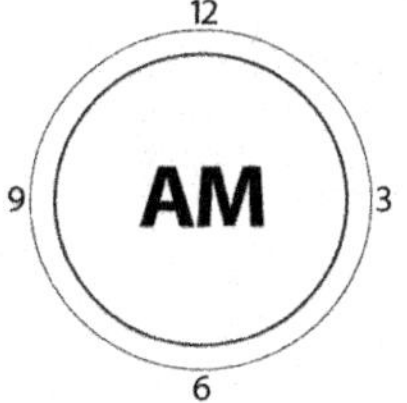
12
9
AM
3
6

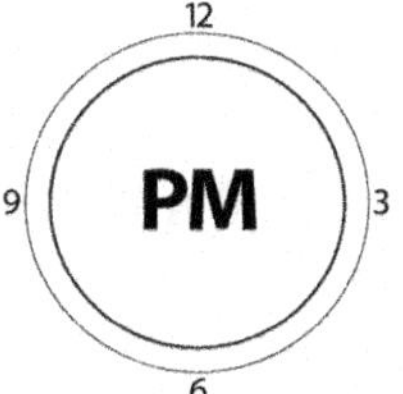
12
9
PM
3
6

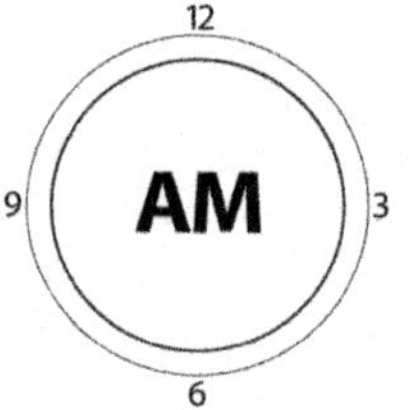
12
9
AM
3
6

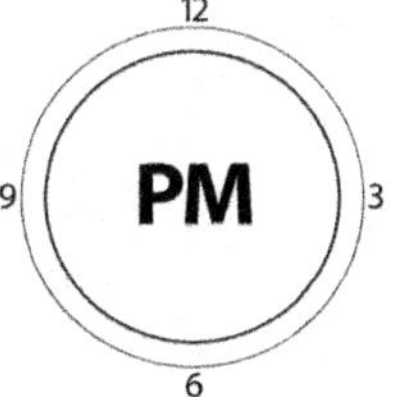
12
9
PM
3
6

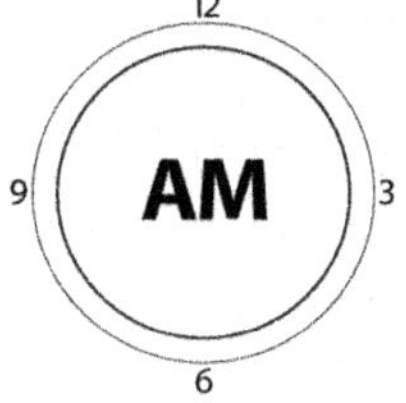
12
9
AM
3
6

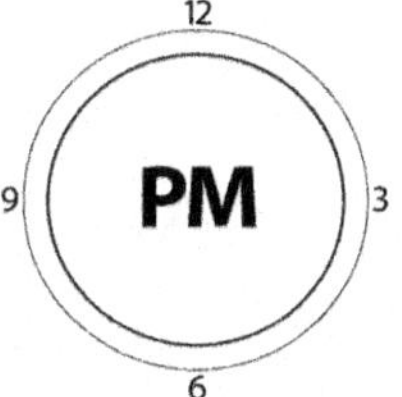
12
9
PM
3
6

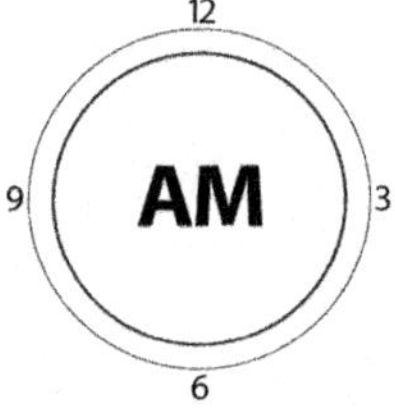
12
9
AM
3
6

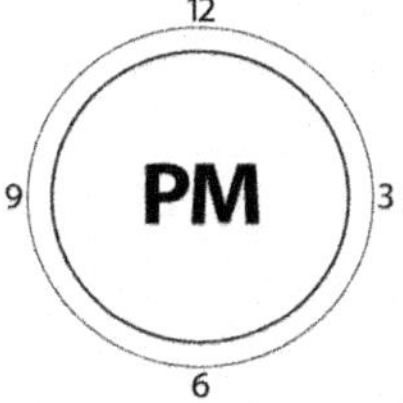
12
9
PM
3
6

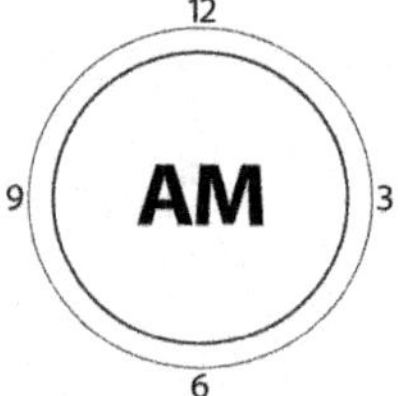
12
9
AM
3
6

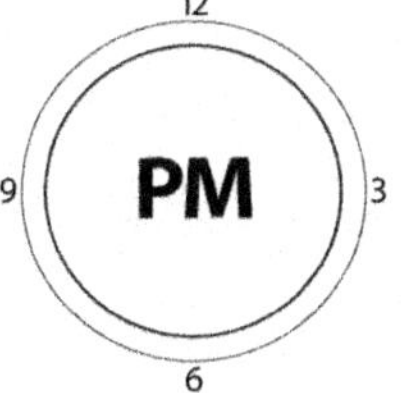
12
9
PM
3
6

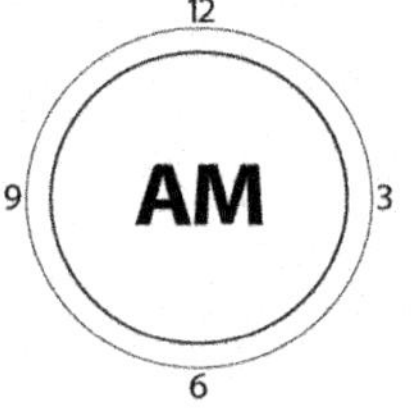
12
9
AM
3
6

12
9
PM
3
6

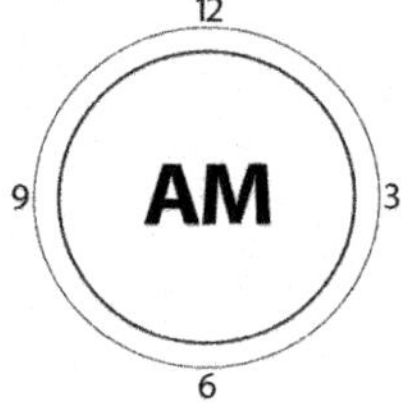
12
9
AM
3
6

12
9
PM
3
6

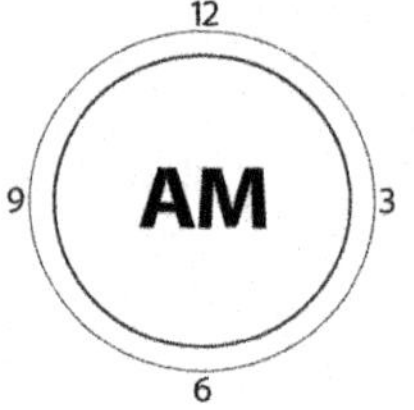
12
9
AM
3
6

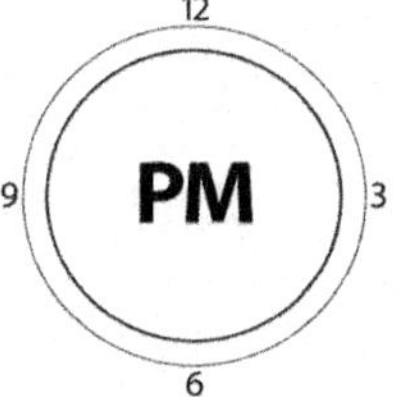
12
9
PM
3
6

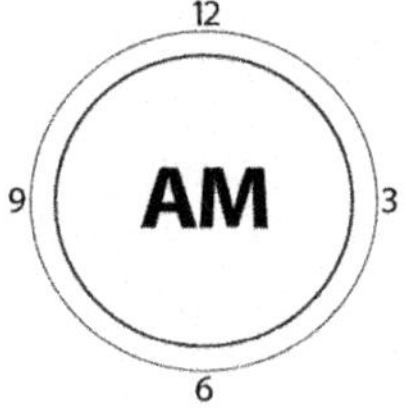
12
9
AM
3
6

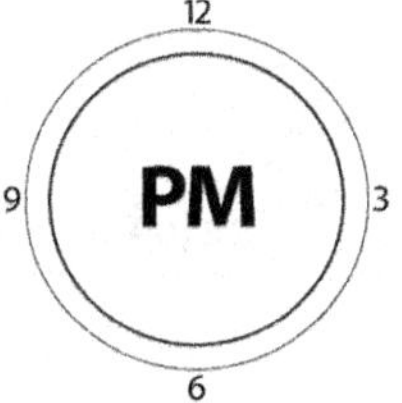
12
9
PM
3
6

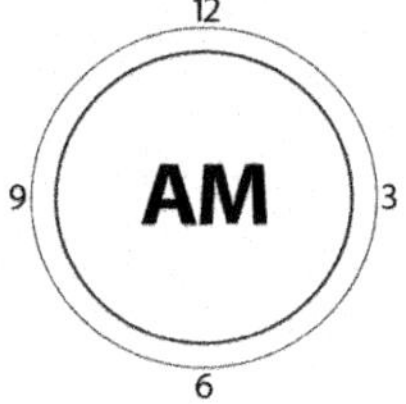
12
9
AM
3
6

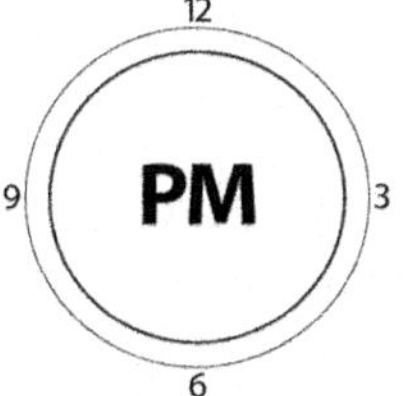
12
9
PM
3
6

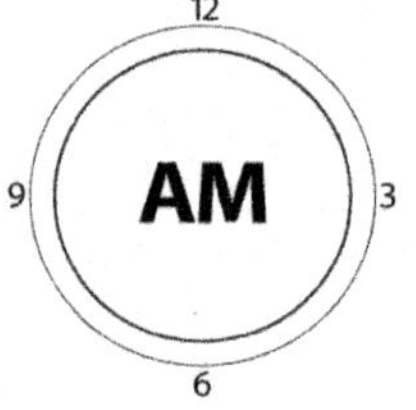
12
9
AM
3
6

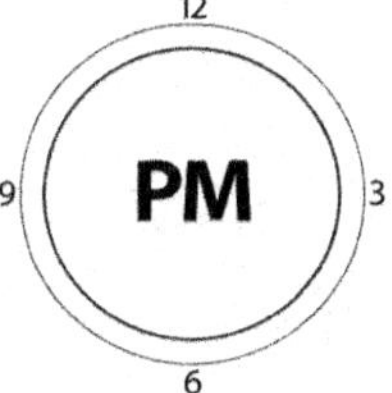
12
9
PM
3
6

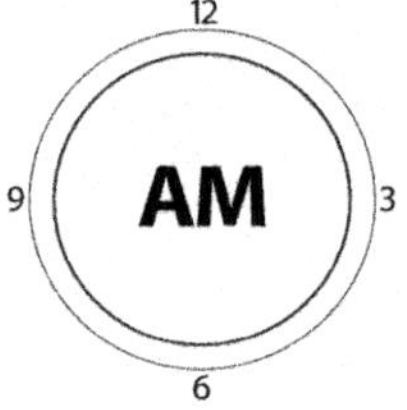
12
9
AM
3
6

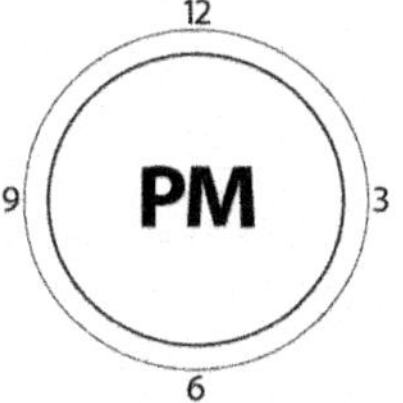
12
9
PM
3
6

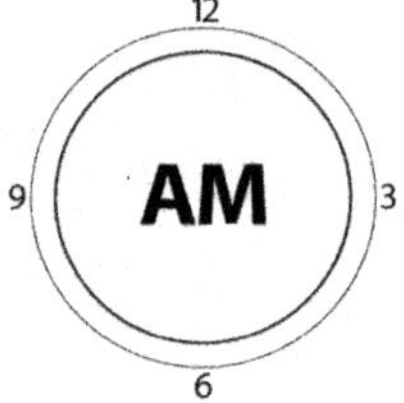
12
9
AM
3
6

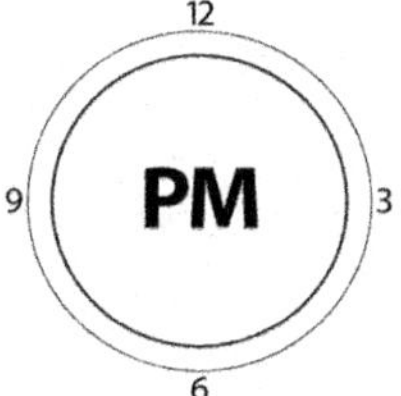
12
9
PM
3
6

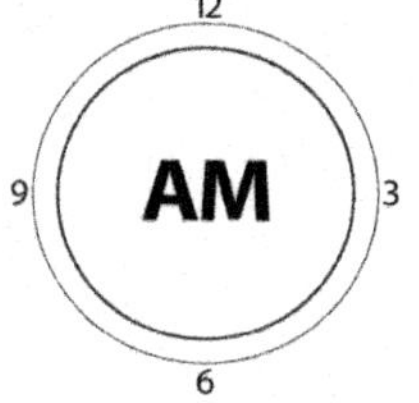
12
9
AM
3
6

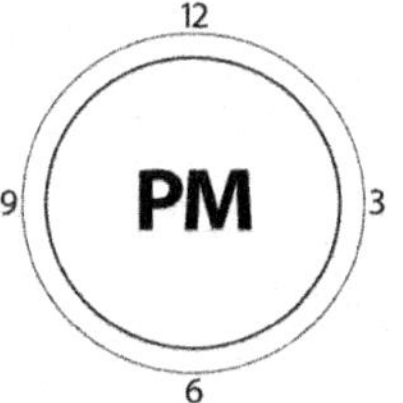
12
9
PM
3
6

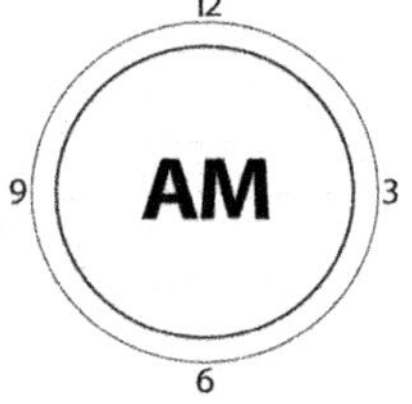
12
9
AM
3
6

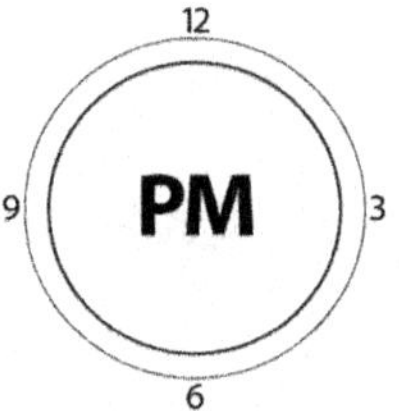
12
9
PM
3
6

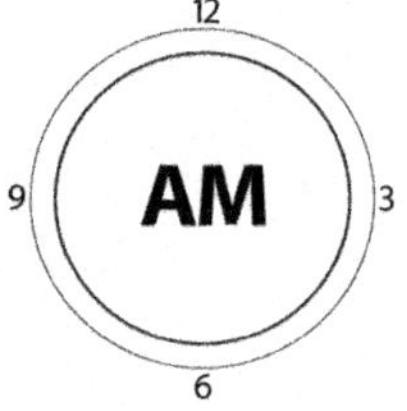
12
9
AM
3
6

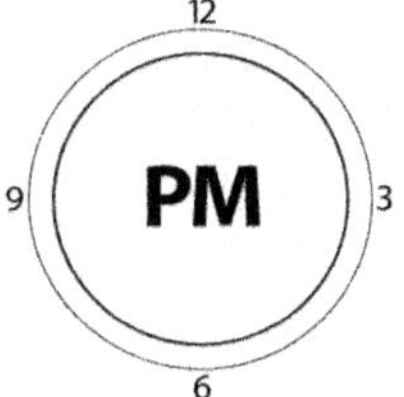
12
9
PM
3
6

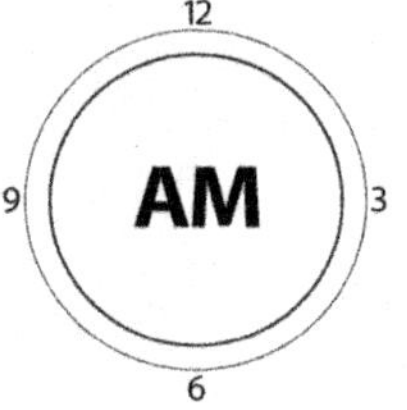
12
9
AM
3
6

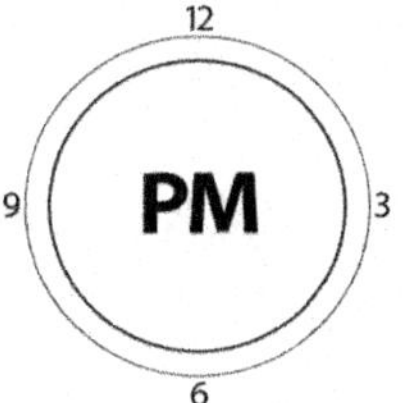
12
9
PM
3
6

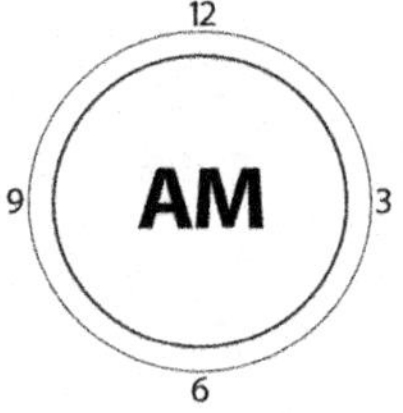
12
9
AM
3
6

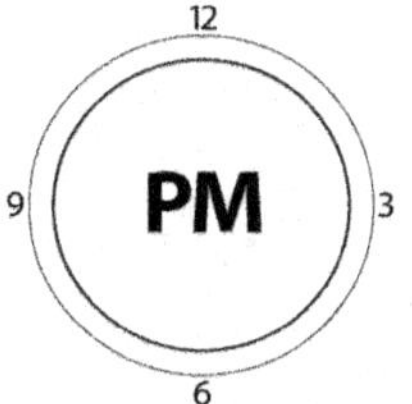
12
9
PM
3
6

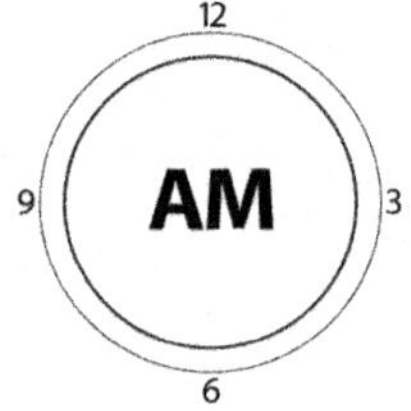
12
9
AM
3
6

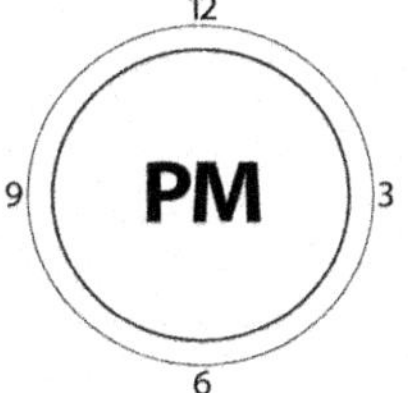
12
9
PM
3
6

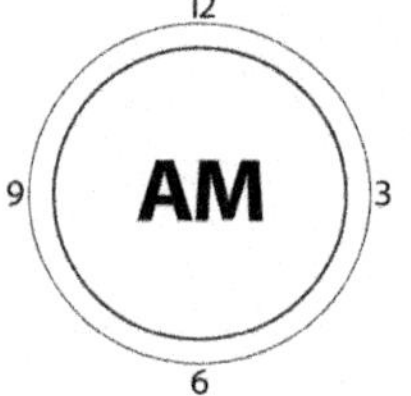
12
9
AM
3
6

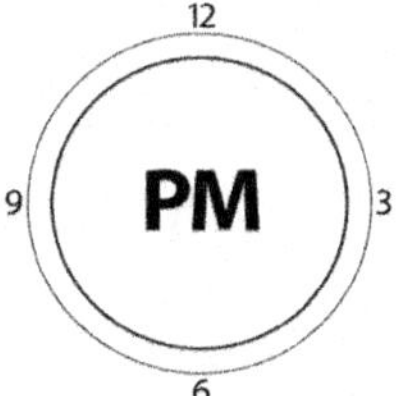
12
9
PM
3
6

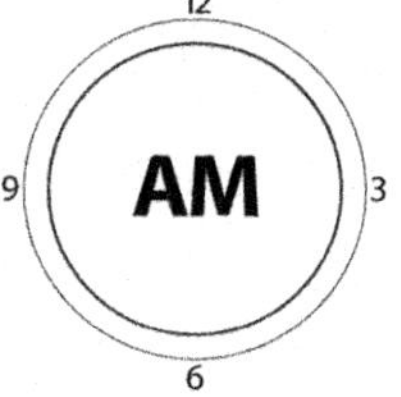
12
9
AM
3
6

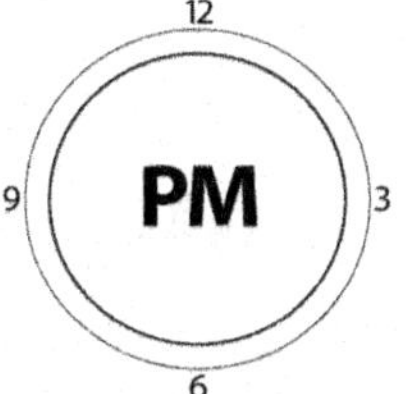
12
9
PM
3
6

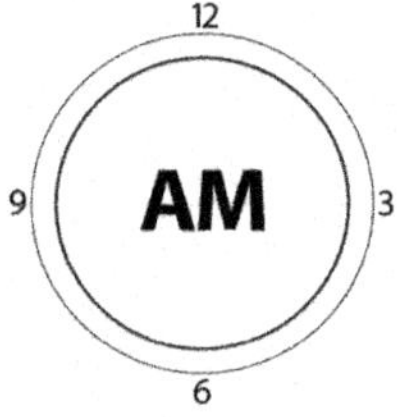
12
9
AM
3
6

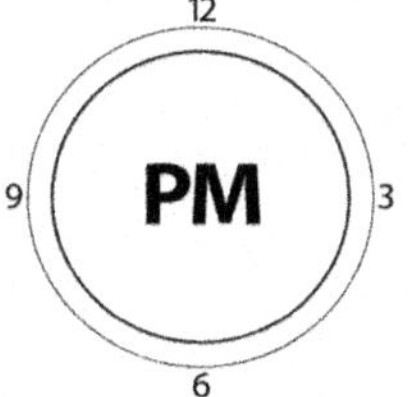
12
9
PM
3
6

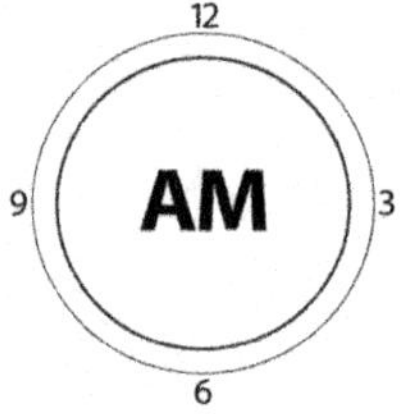
12
9
AM
3
6

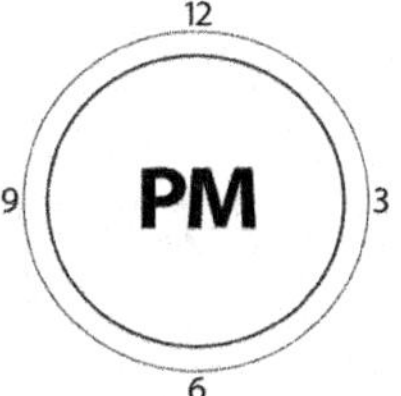
12
9
PM
3
6

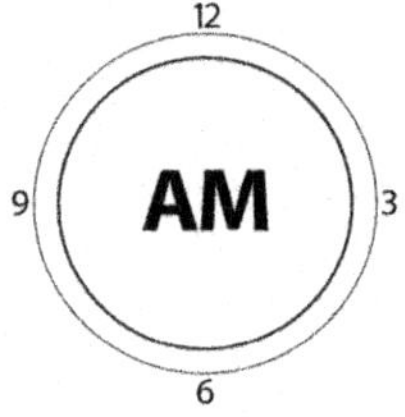
12
9
AM
3
6

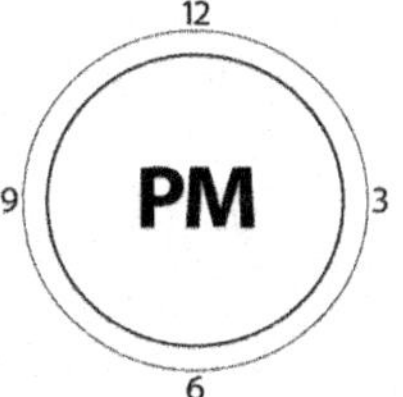
12
9
PM
3
6

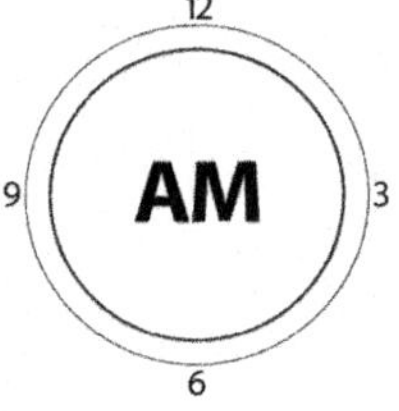
12
9
AM
3
6

12
9
PM
3
6

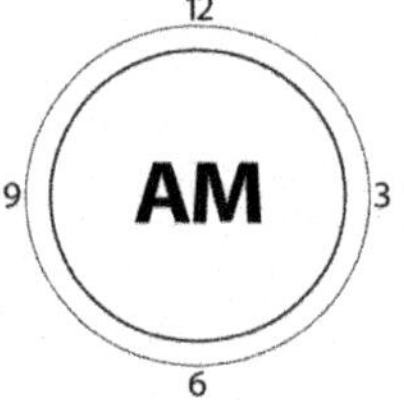
12
9
AM
3
6

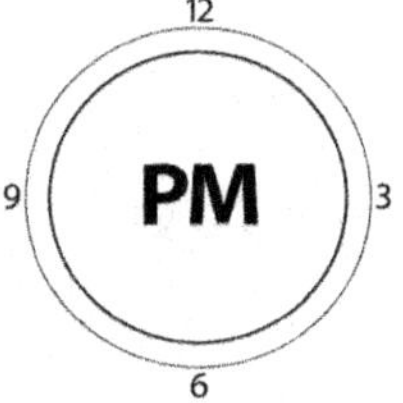
12
9
PM
3
6

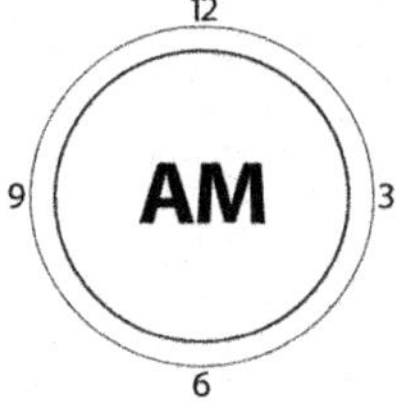
12
9
AM
3
6

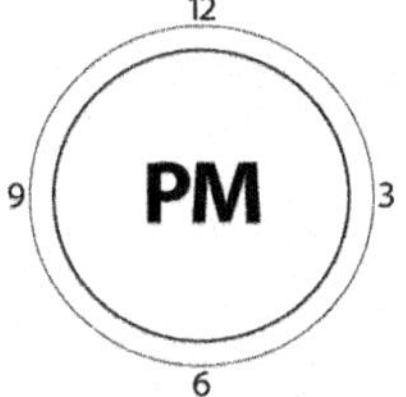
12
9
PM
3
6

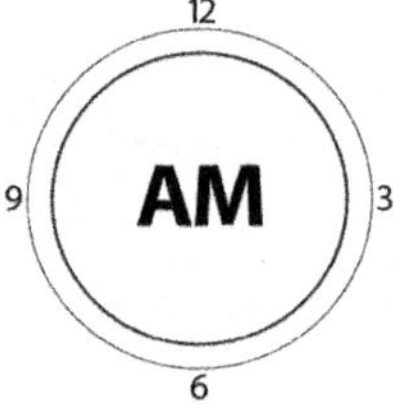
12
9
AM
3
6

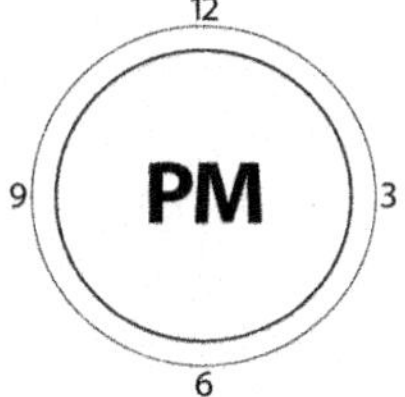
12
9
PM
3
6

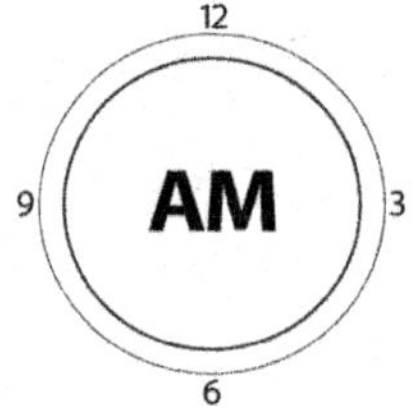
12
9
AM
3
6

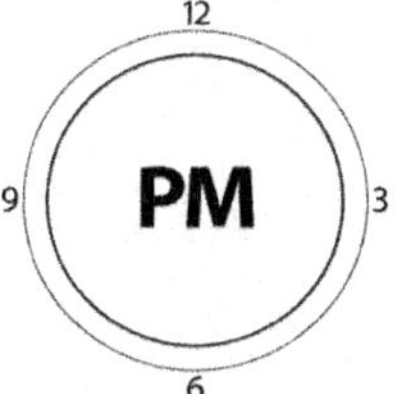
12
9
PM
3
6

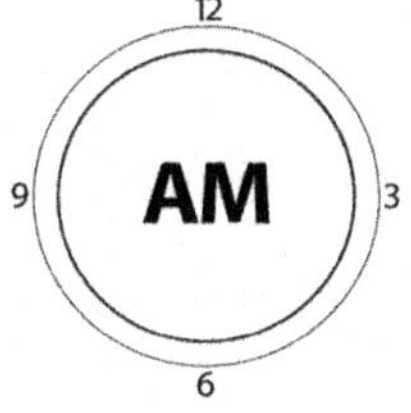
12
9
AM
3
6

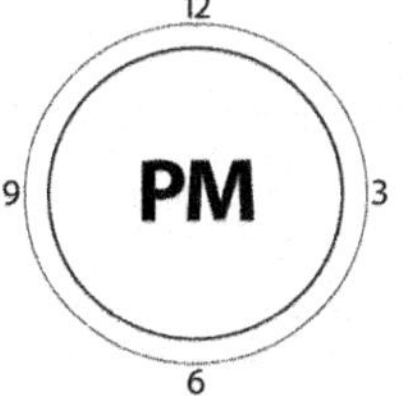
12
9
PM
3
6

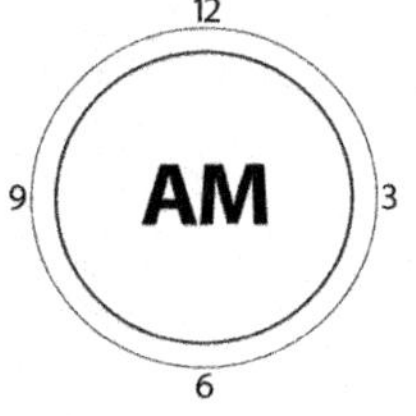
12
9
AM
3
6

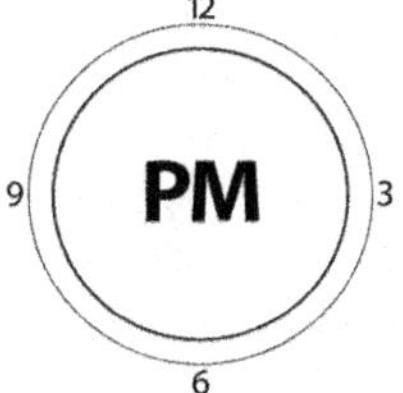
12
9
PM
3
6

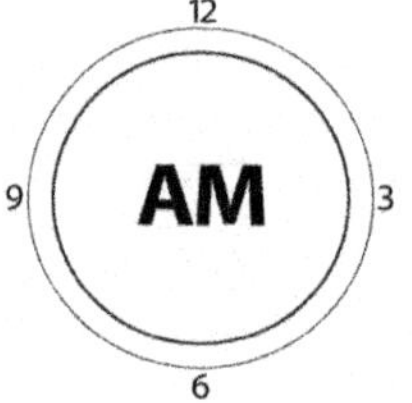
12
9
AM
3
6

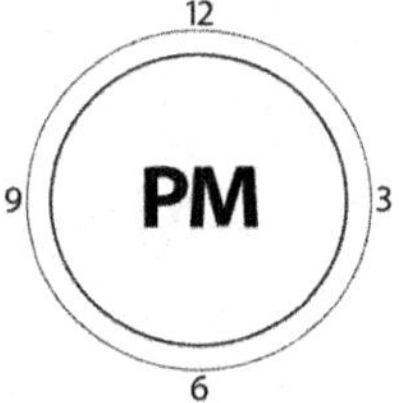
12
9
PM
3
6

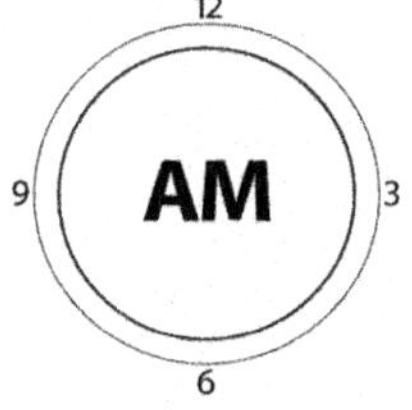
12
9
AM
3
6

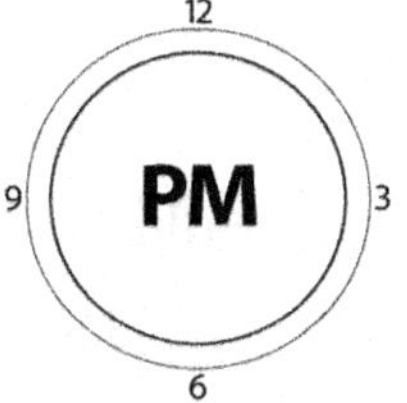
12
9
PM
3
6

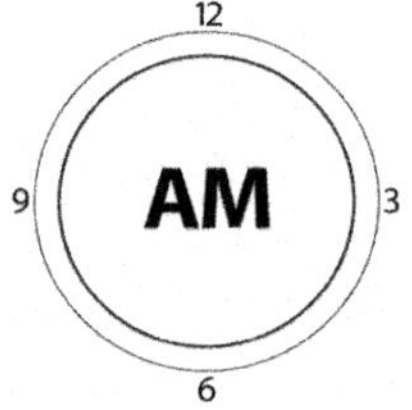
12
9
AM
3
6

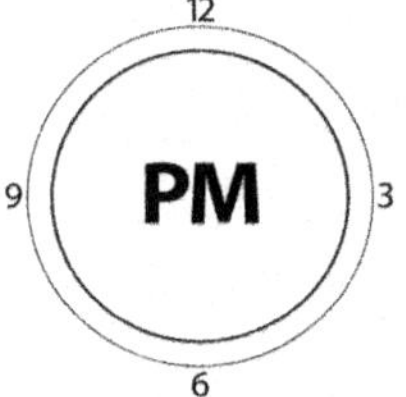
12
9
PM
3
6

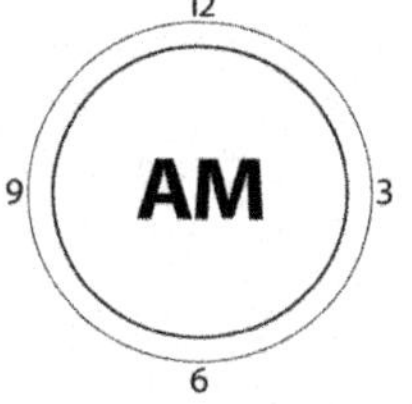
12
9
AM
3
6

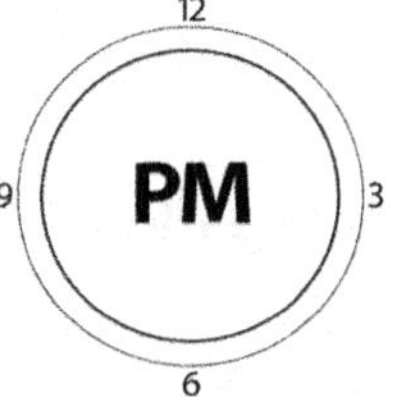
12
9
PM
3
6

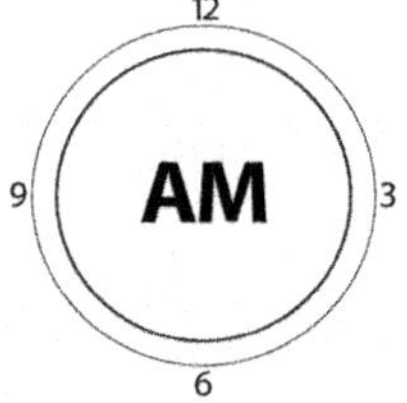
12
9
AM
3
6

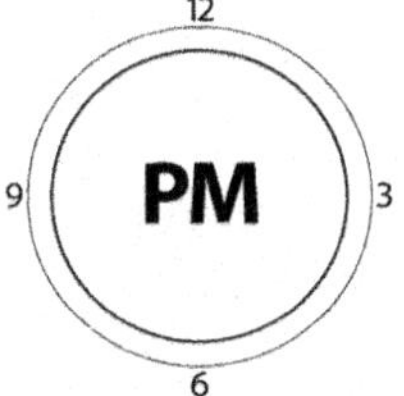
12
9
PM
3
6

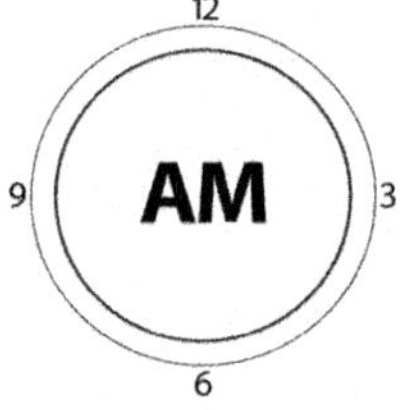
12
9
AM
3
6

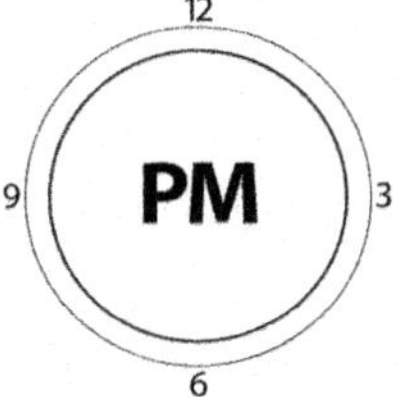
12
9
PM
3
6

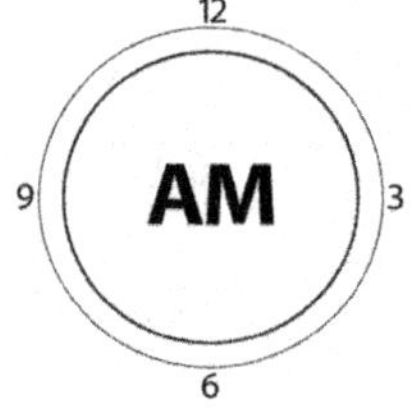
12
9
AM
3
6

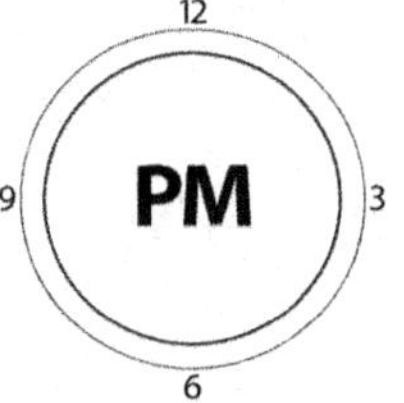
12
9
PM
3
6

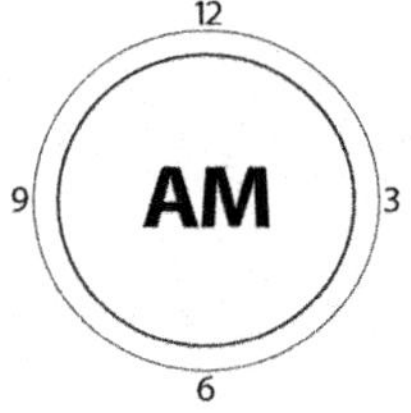
12
9
AM
3
6

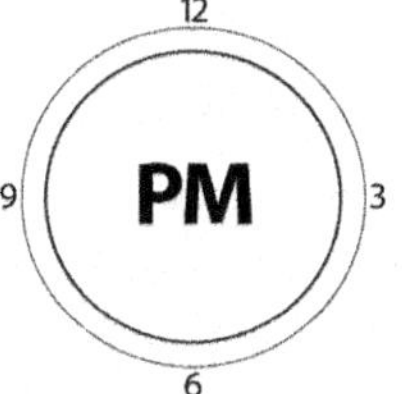
12
9
PM
3
6

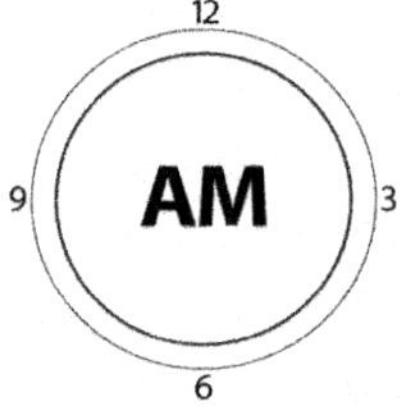
12
9
AM
3
6

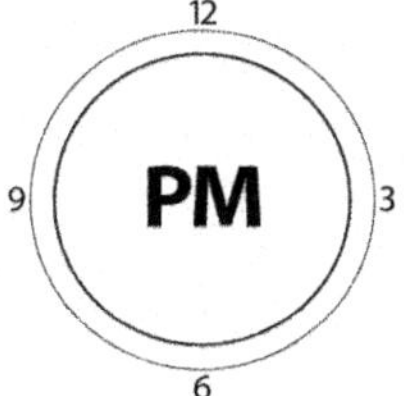
12
9
PM
3
6

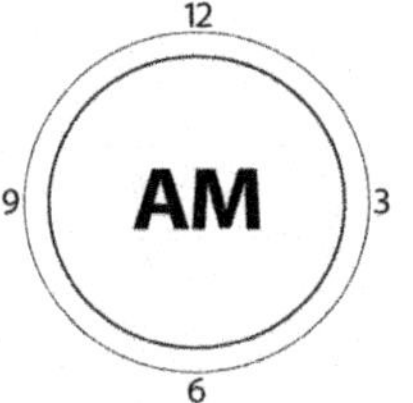
12
9
AM
3
6

12
9
PM
3
6

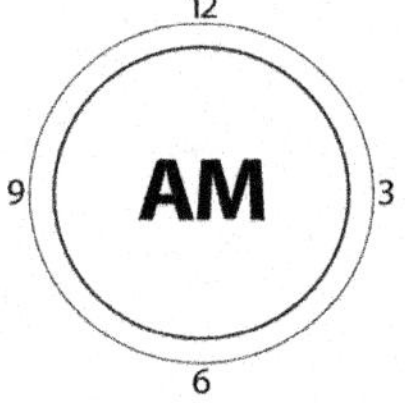
12
9
AM
3
6

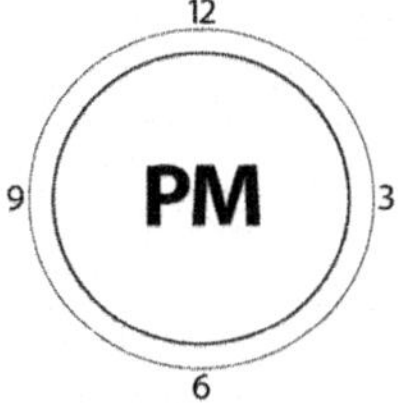
12
9
PM
3
6

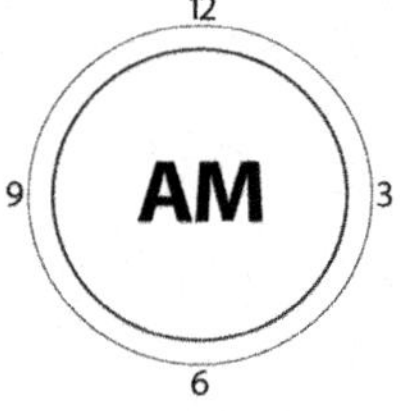
12
9
AM
3
6

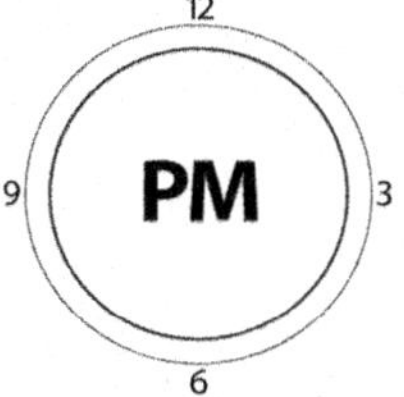
12
9
PM
3
6

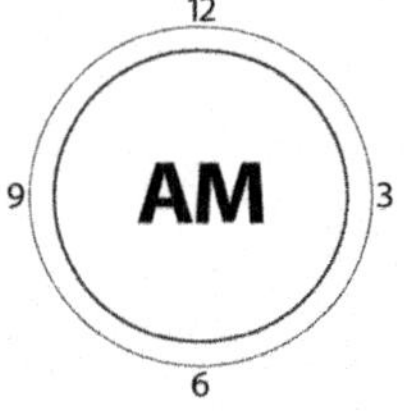
12
9
AM
3
6

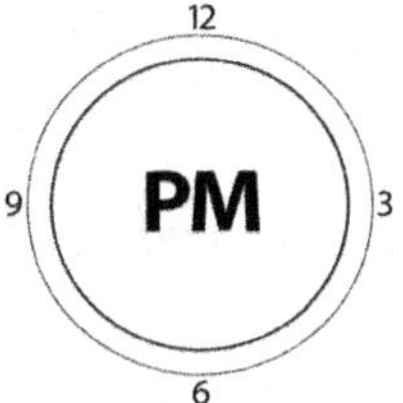
12
9
PM
3
6

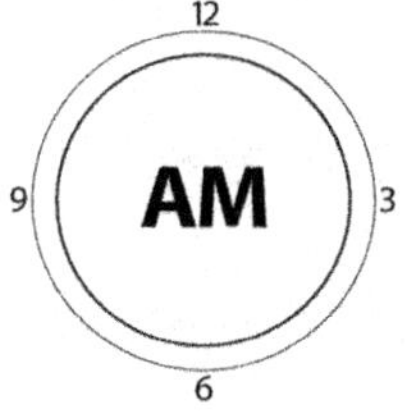
12
9
AM
3
6

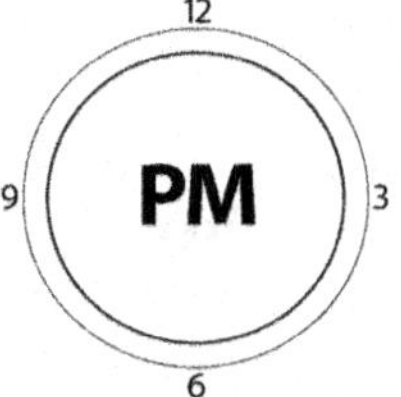
12
9
PM
3
6

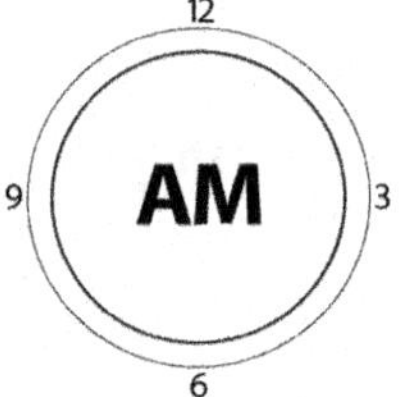
12
9
AM
3
6

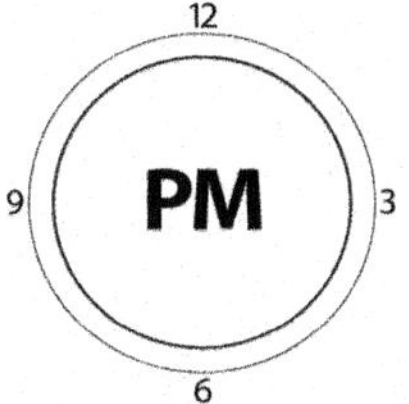
12
9
PM
3
6

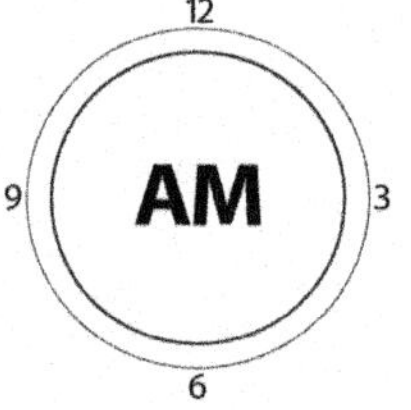
12
9
AM
3
6

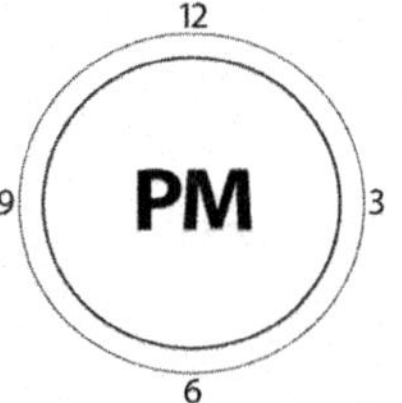
12
9
PM
3
6

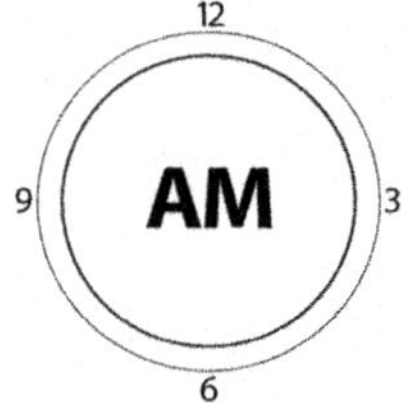
12
9
AM
3
6

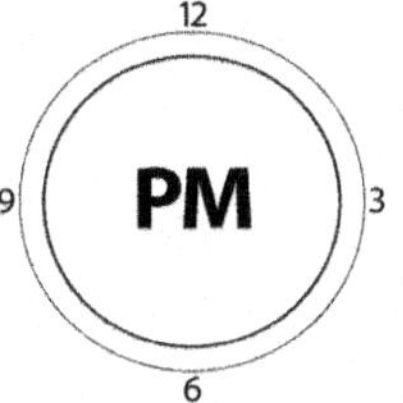
12
9
PM
3
6

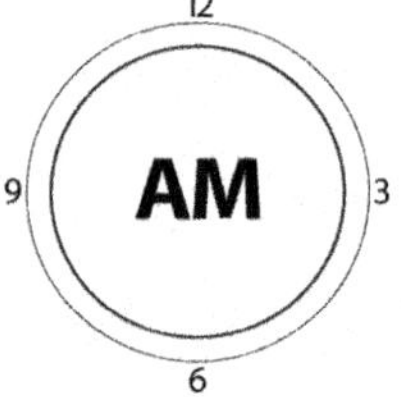
12
9
AM
3
6

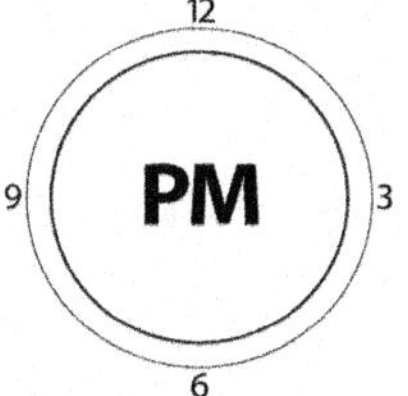
12
9
PM
3
6

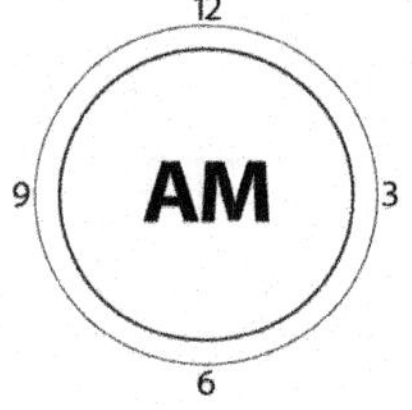
12
9
AM
3
6

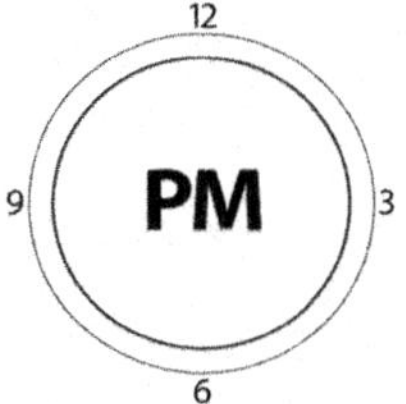
12
9
PM
3
6

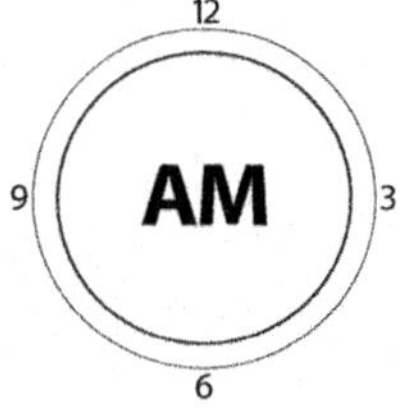
12
9
AM
3
6

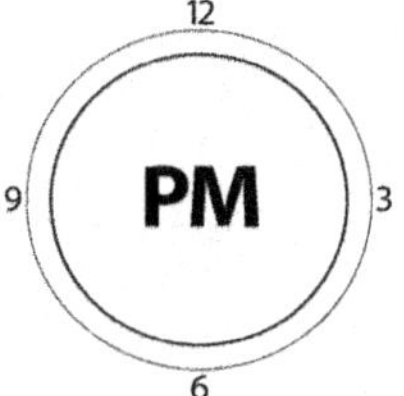
12
9
PM
3
6

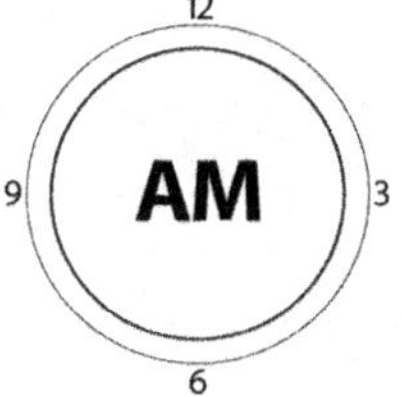
12
9
AM
3
6

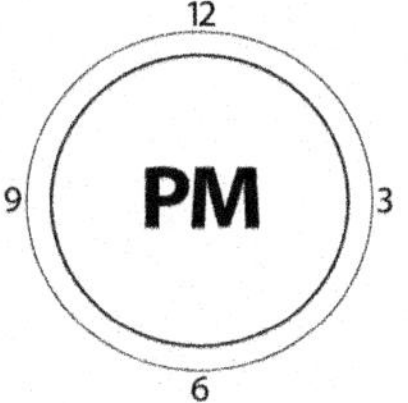
12
9
PM
3
6

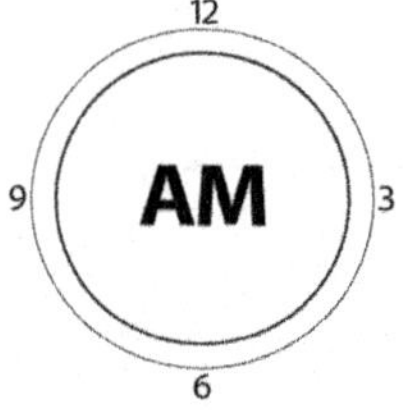
12
9
AM
3
6

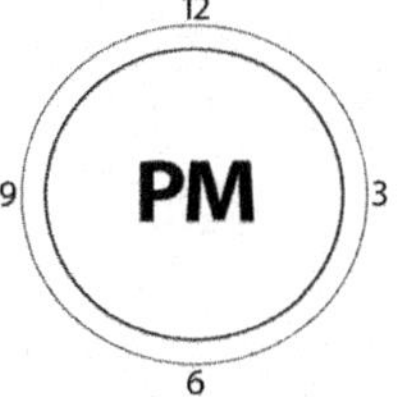
12
9
PM
3
6

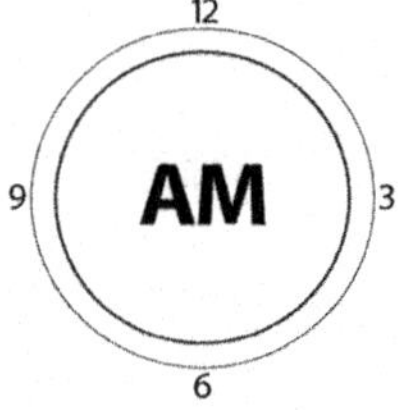
12
9
AM
3
6

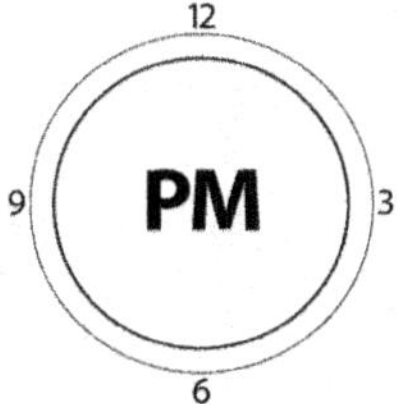
12
9
PM
3
6

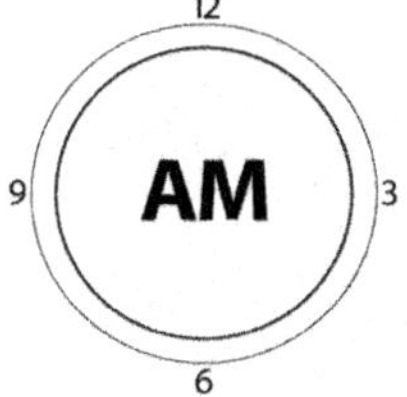
12
9
AM
3
6

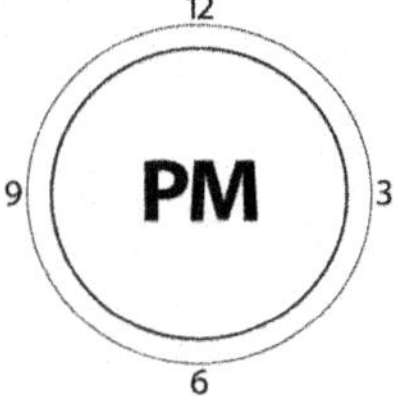
12
9
PM
3
6

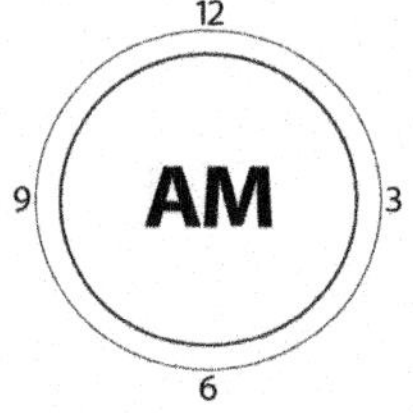
12
9
AM
3
6

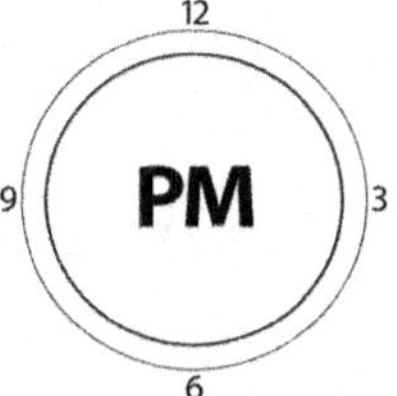
12
9
PM
3
6

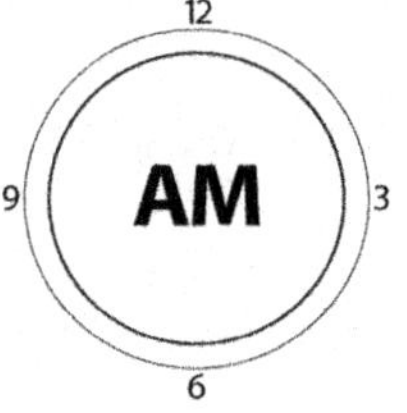
12
9
AM
3
6

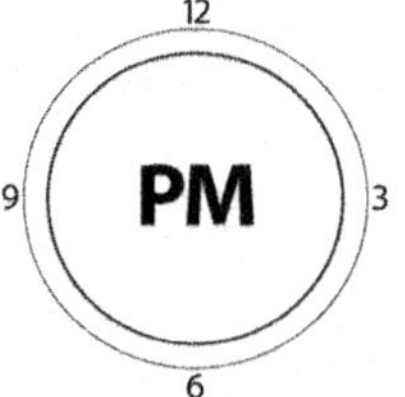
12
9
PM
3
6

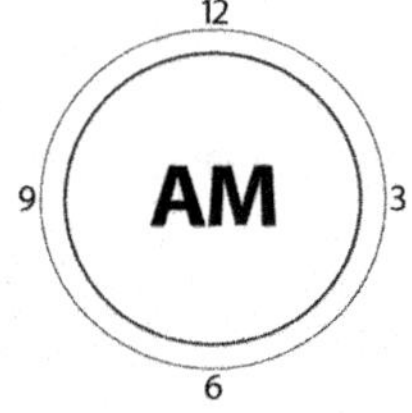
12
9
AM
3
6

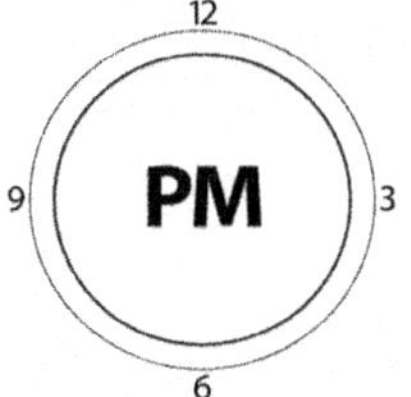
12
9
PM
3
6

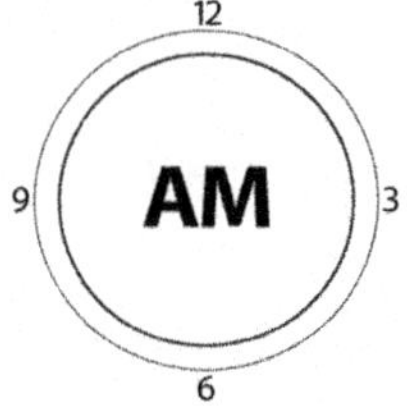
12
9
AM
3
6

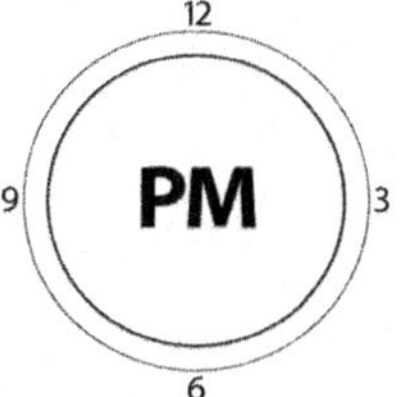
12
9
PM
3
6

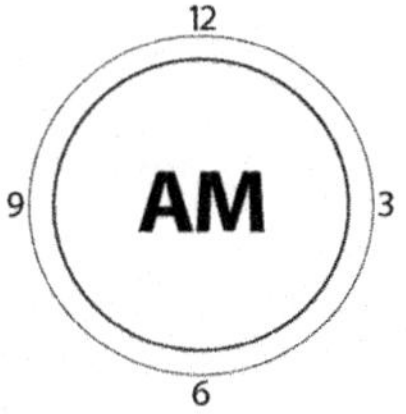
12
9
AM
3
6

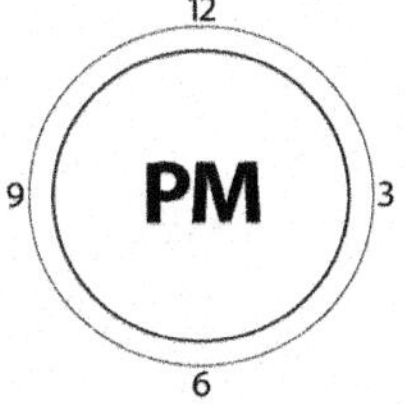
12
9
PM
3
6

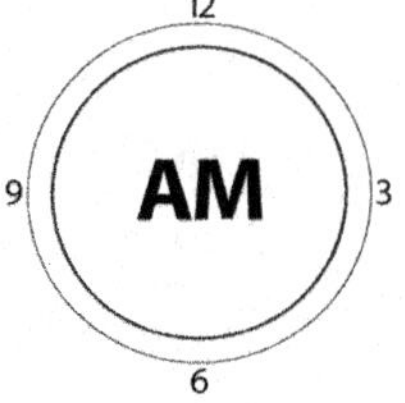
12
9
AM
3
6

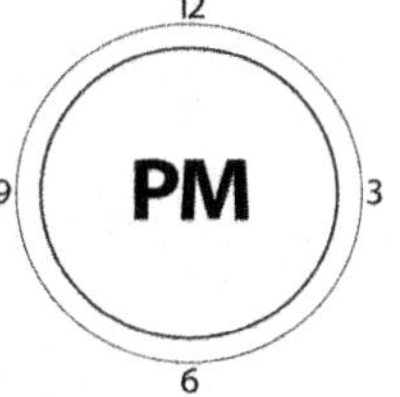
12
9
PM
3
6

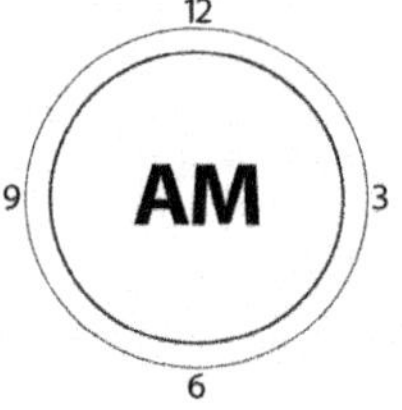
12
9
AM
3
6

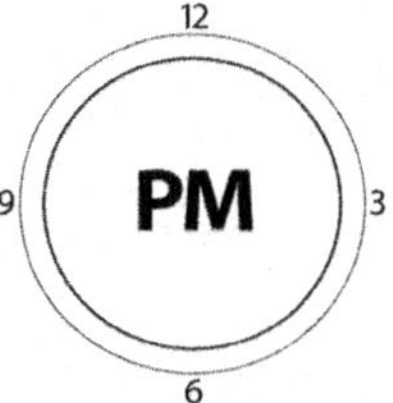
12
9
PM
3
6

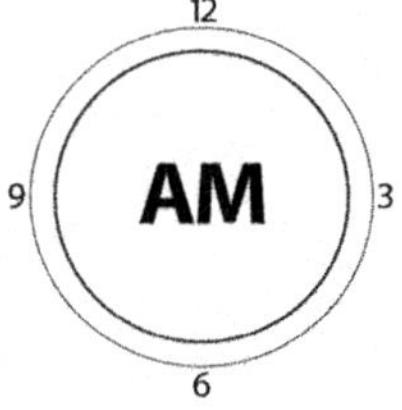
12
9
AM
3
6

12
9
PM
3
6

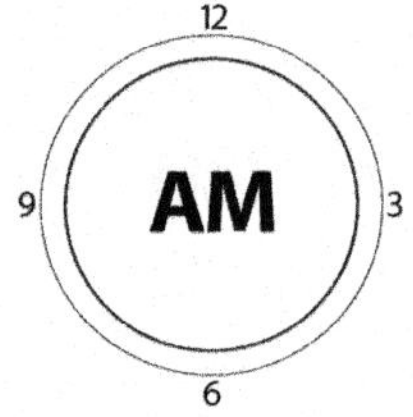
12
9
AM
3
6

12
9
PM
3
6

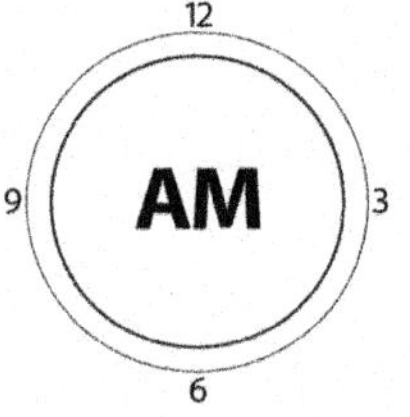
12
9
AM
3
6

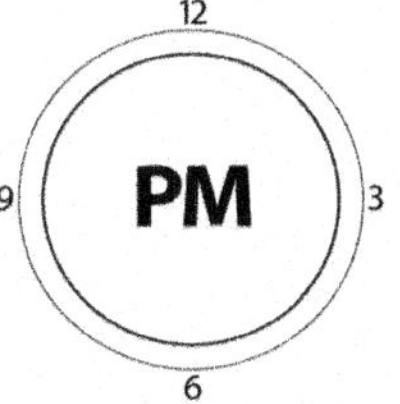
12
9
PM
3
6

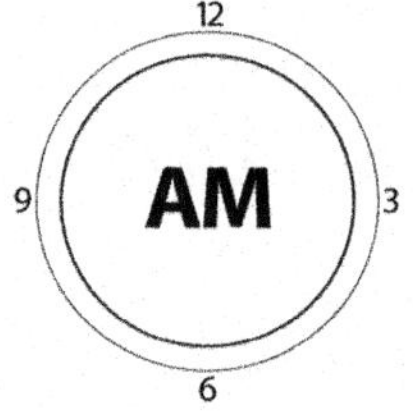
12
9
AM
3
6

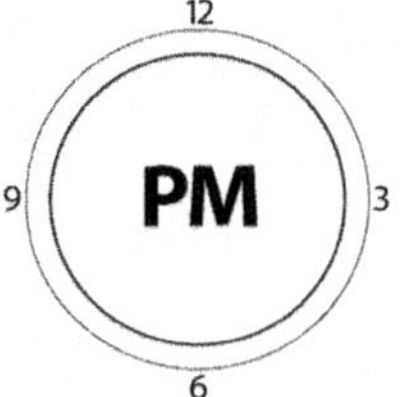
12
9
PM
3
6

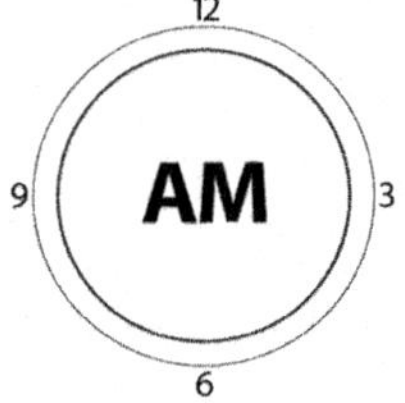
12
9
AM
3
6

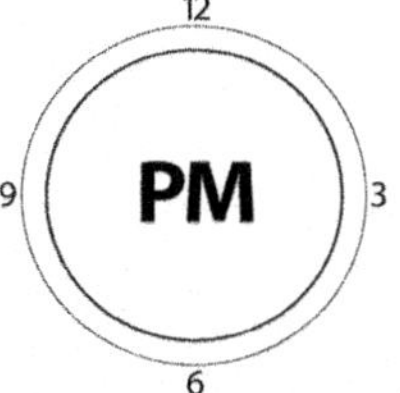
12
9
PM
3
6

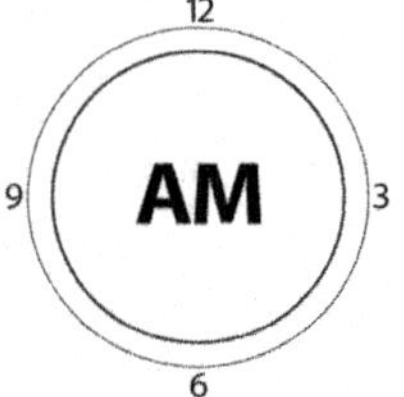
12
9
AM
3
6

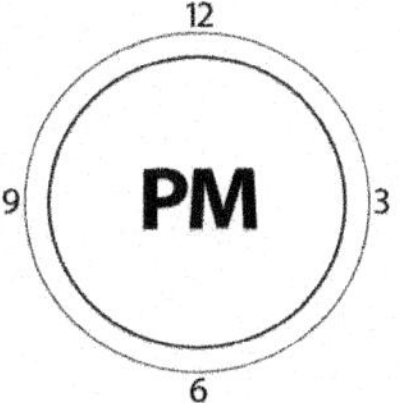
12
9
PM
3
6

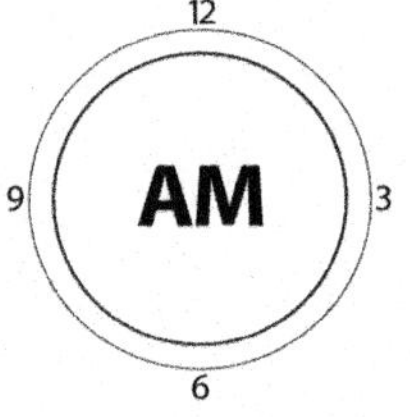
12
9
AM
3
6

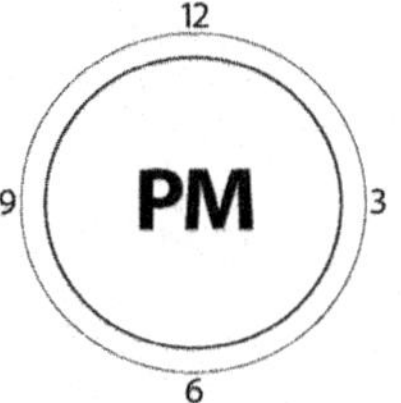
12
9
PM
3
6

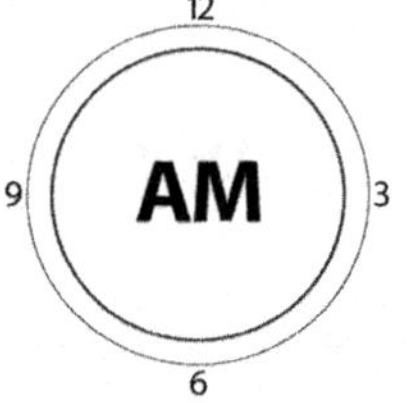
12
9
AM
3
6

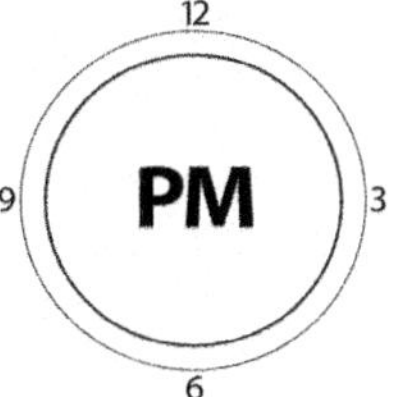
12
9
PM
3
6

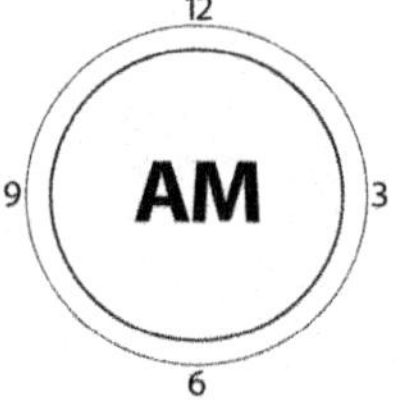
12
9
AM
3
6

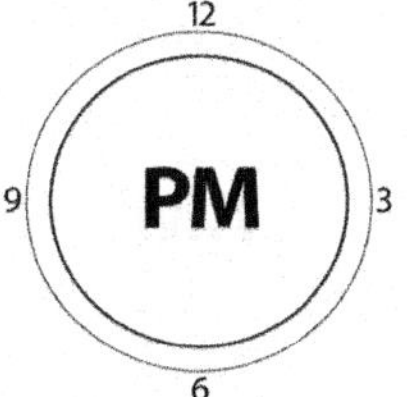
12
9
PM
3
6

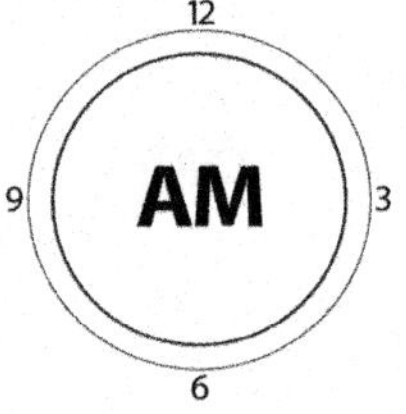
12
9
AM
3
6

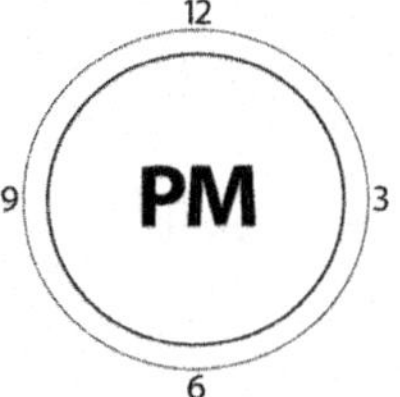
12
9
PM
3
6

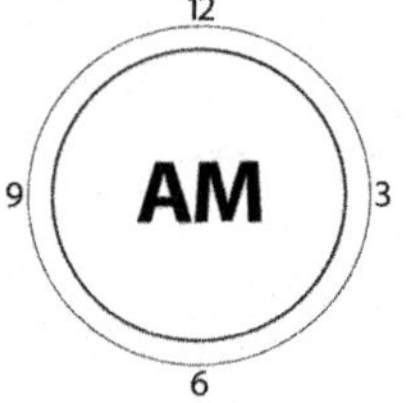
12
9
AM
3
6

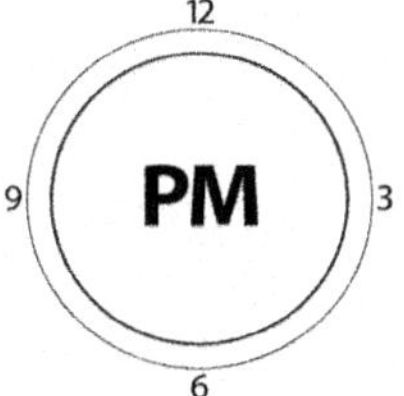
12
9
PM
3
6

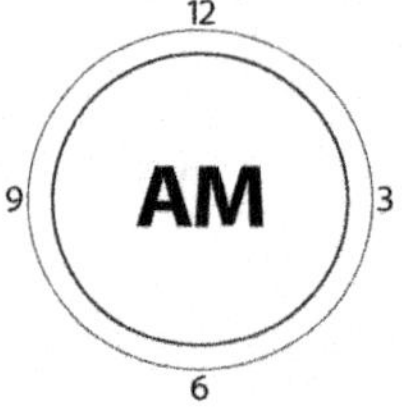
12
9
AM
3
6

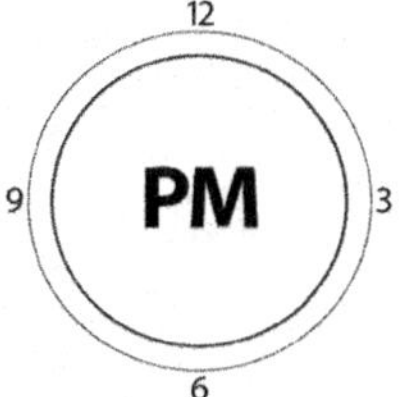
12
9
PM
3
6

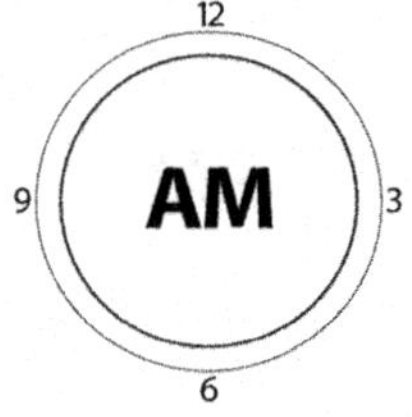
12
9
AM
3
6

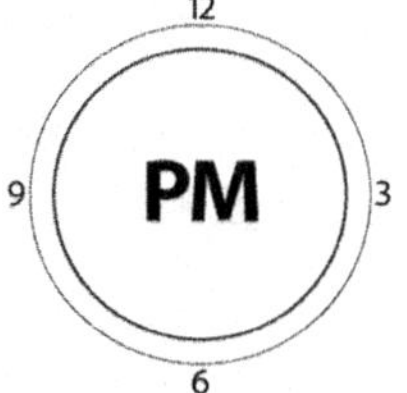
12
9
PM
3
6

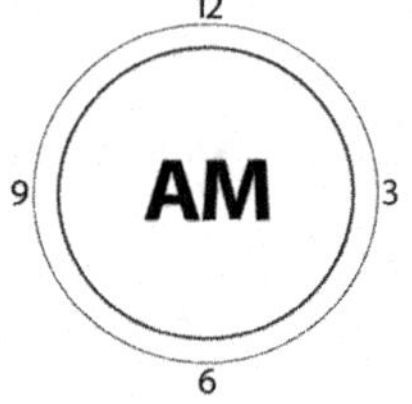
12
9
AM
3
6

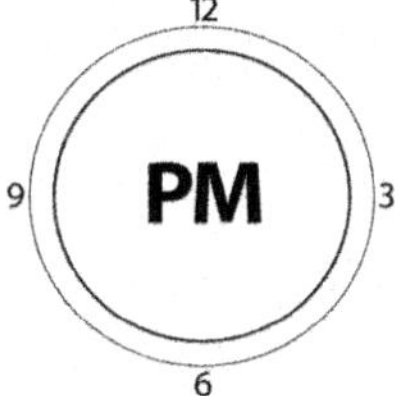
12
9
PM
3
6

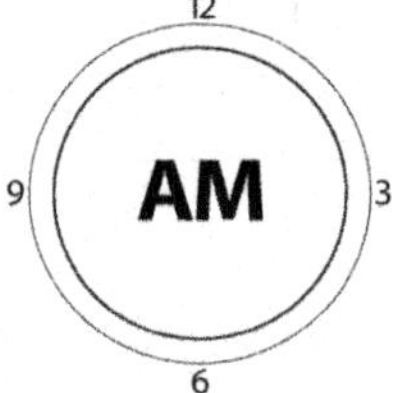
12
9
AM
3
6

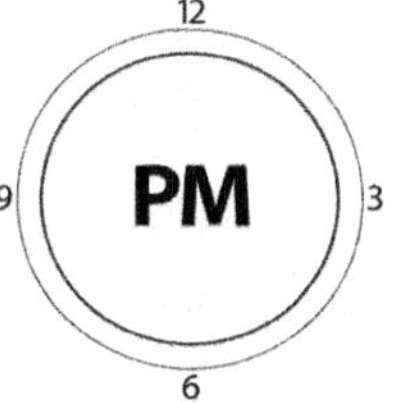
12
9
PM
3
6

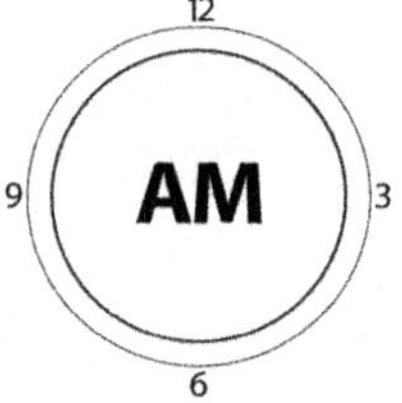
12
9
AM
3
6

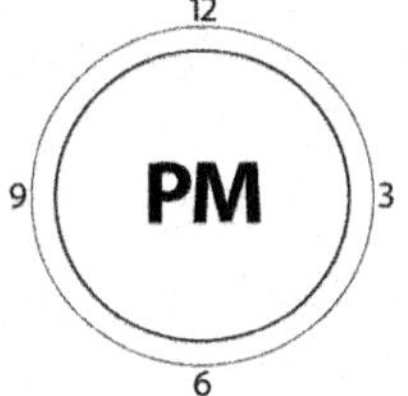
12
9
PM
3
6

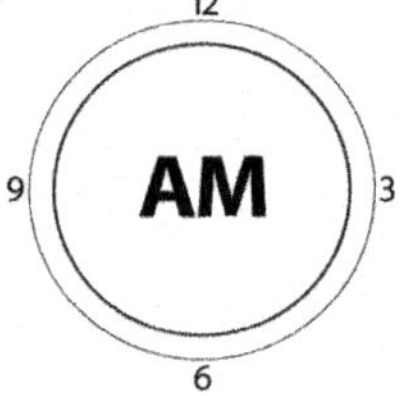
12
9
AM
3
6

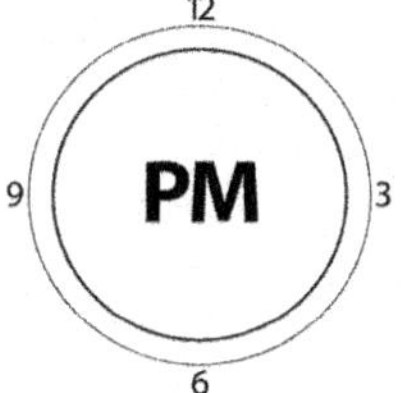
12
9
PM
3
6

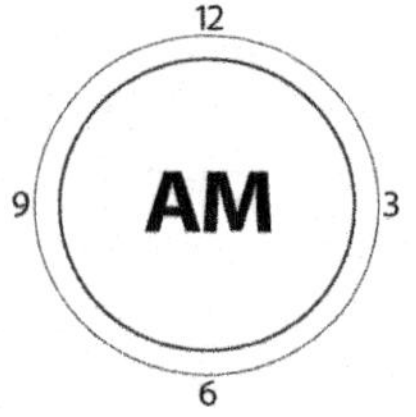
12
9
AM
3
6

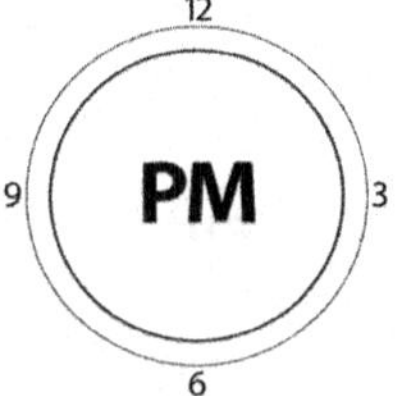
12
9
PM
3
6

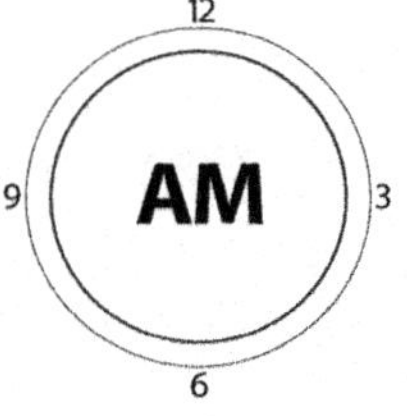
12
9
AM
3
6

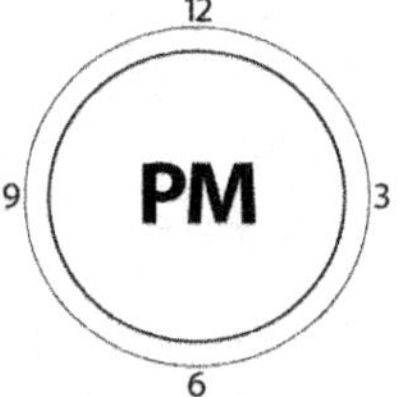
12
9
PM
3
6

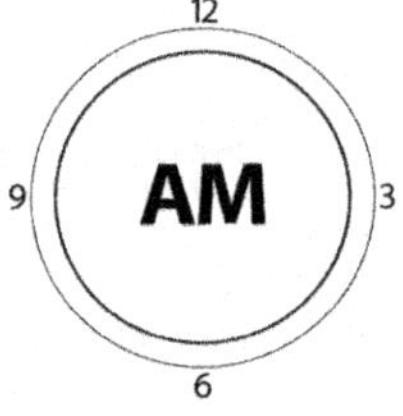
12
9
AM
3
6

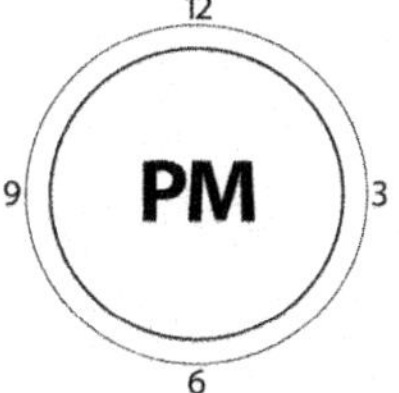
12
9
PM
3
6

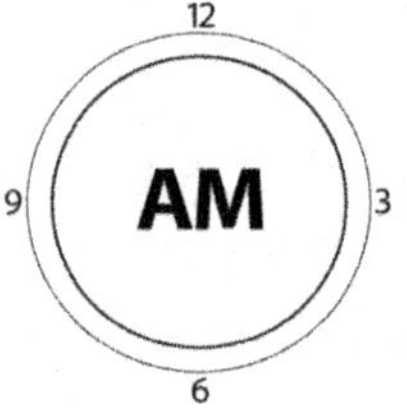
12
9
AM
3
6

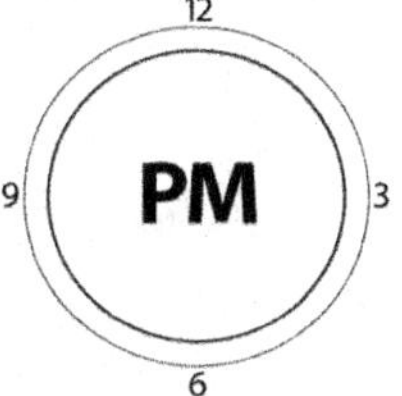
12
9
PM
3
6

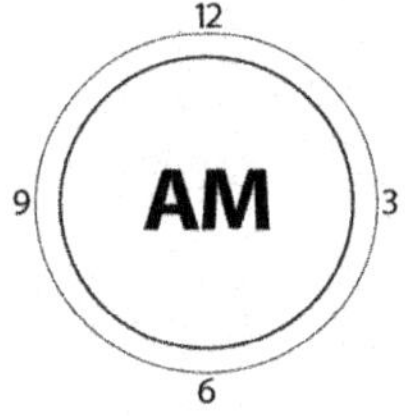
12
9
AM
3
6

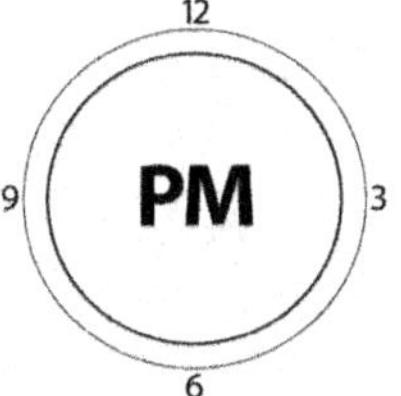
12
9
PM
3
6

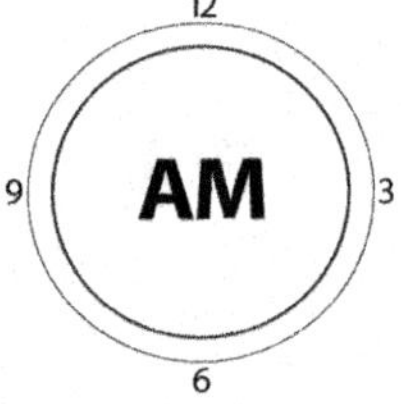
12
9
AM
3
6

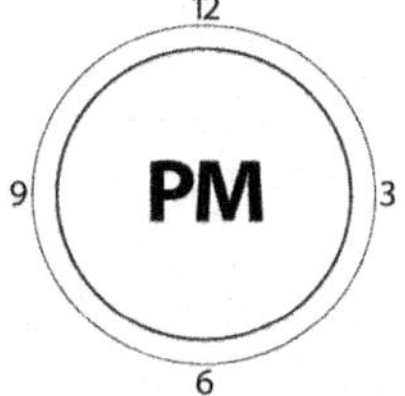
12
9
PM
3
6

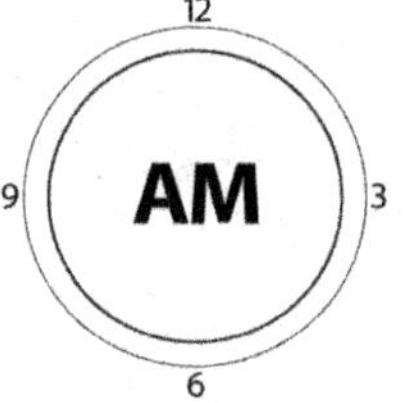
12
9
AM
3
6

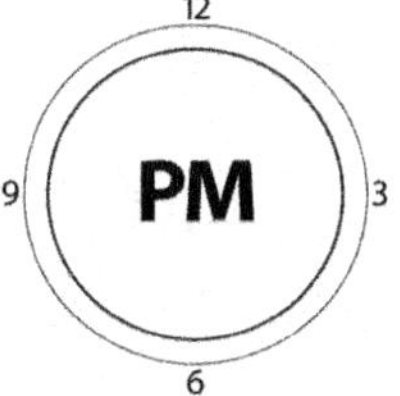
12
9
PM
3
6

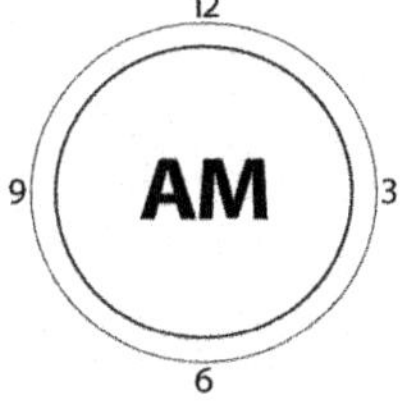
12
9
AM
3
6

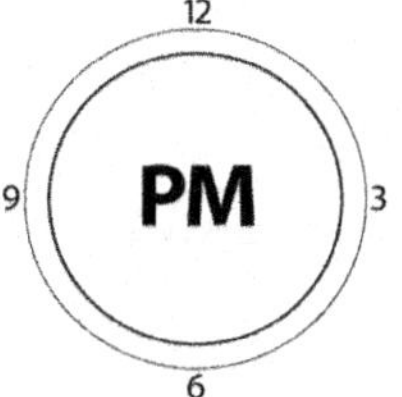
12
9
PM
3
6

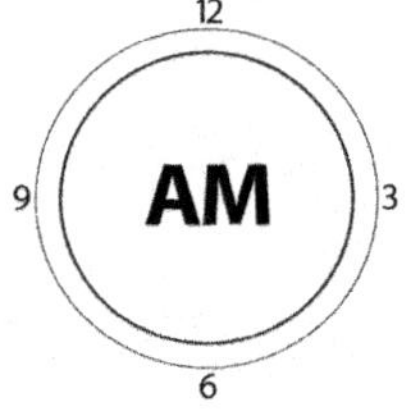
12
9
AM
3
6

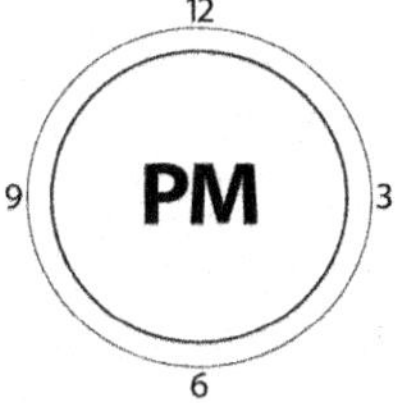
12
9
PM
3
6

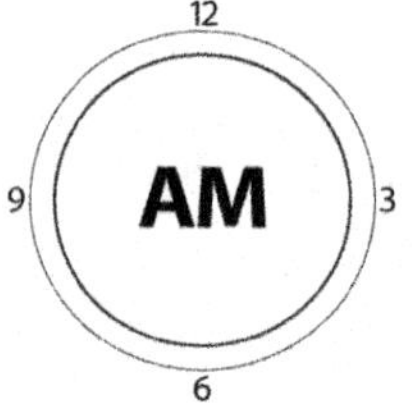
12
9
AM
3
6

12
9
PM
3
6

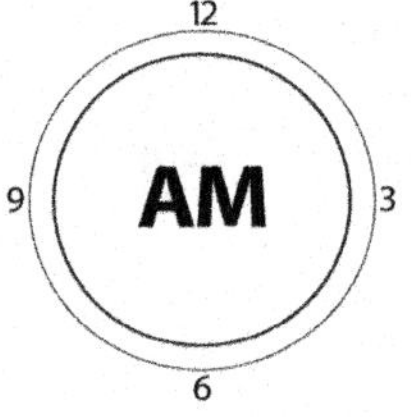
12
9
AM
3
6

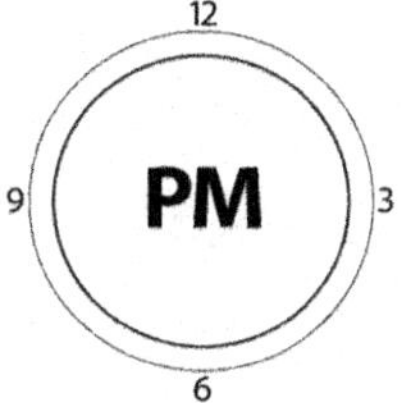
12
9
PM
3
6

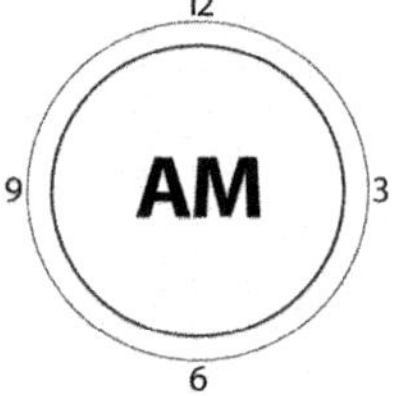
12
9
AM
3
6

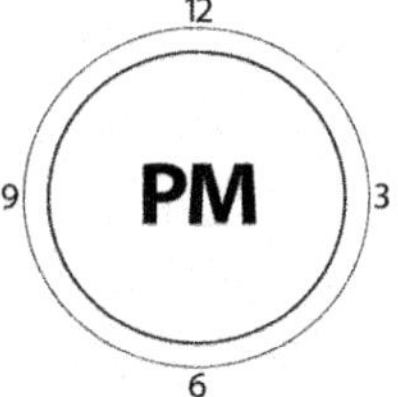
12
9
PM
3
6

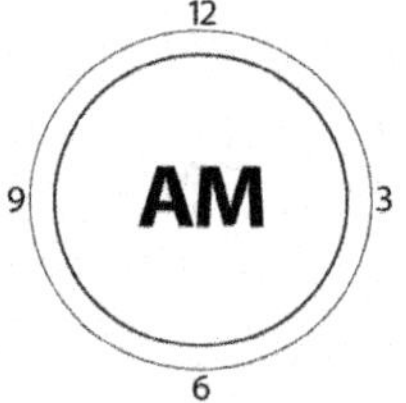
12
9
AM
3
6

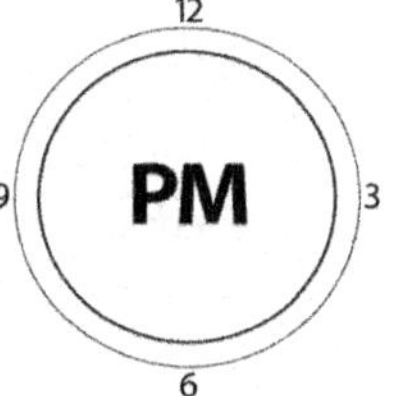
12
9
PM
3
6

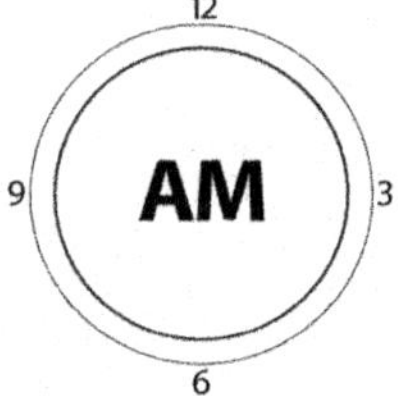
12
9
AM
3
6

12
9
PM
3
6

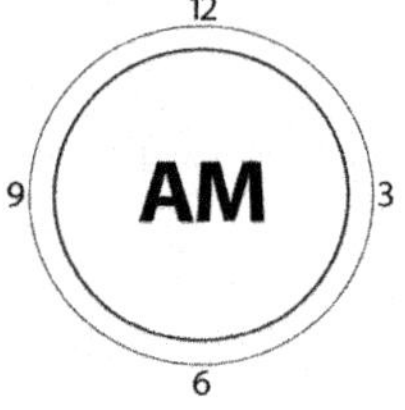
12
9
AM
3
6

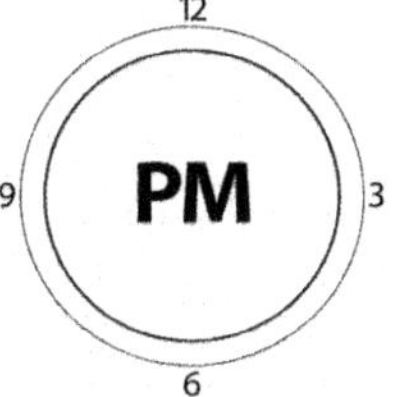
12
9
PM
3
6

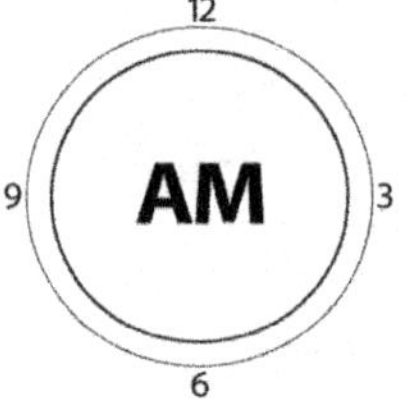
12
9
AM
3
6

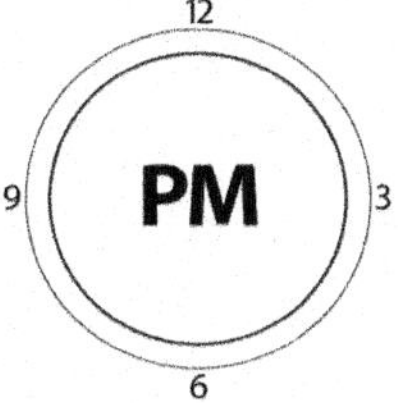
12
9
PM
3
6

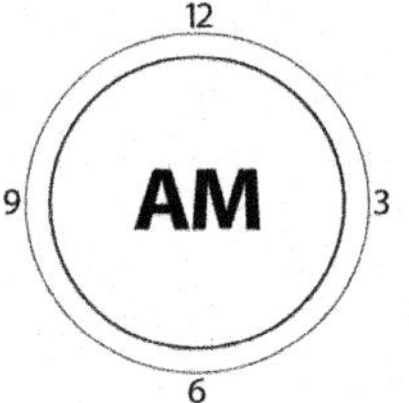
12
9
AM
3
6

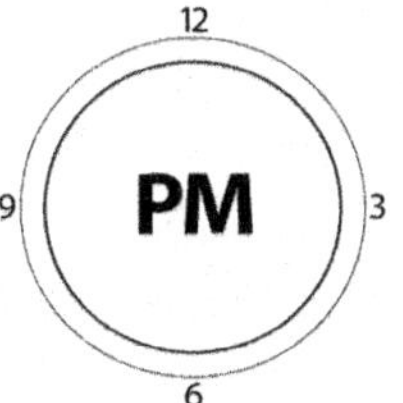
12
9
PM
3
6

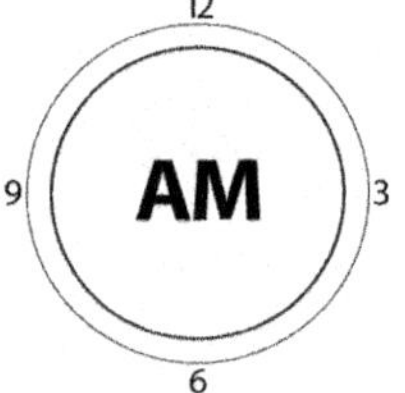
12
9
AM
3
6

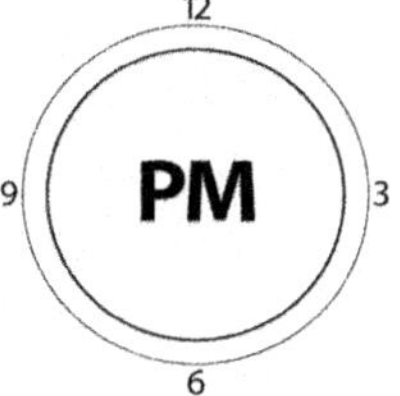
12
9
PM
3
6

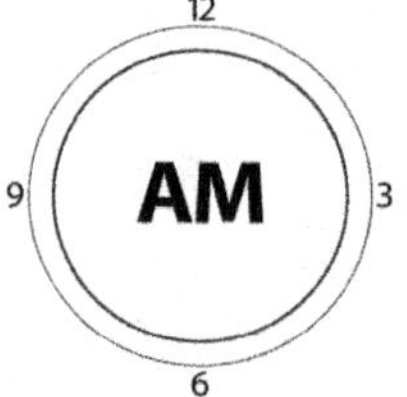
12
9
AM
3
6

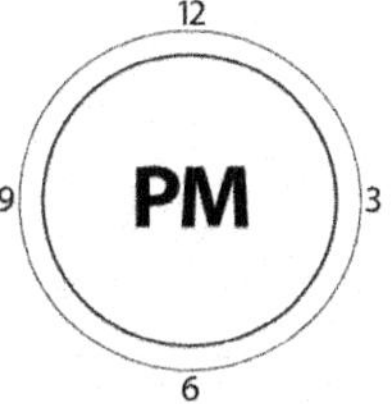
12
9
PM
3
6

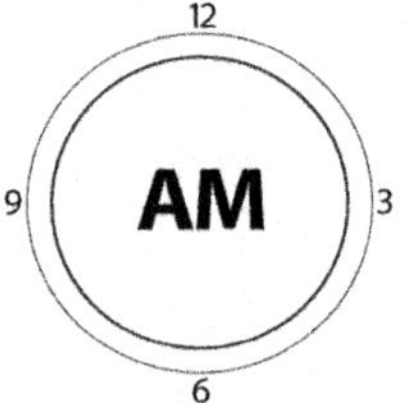
12
9
AM
3
6

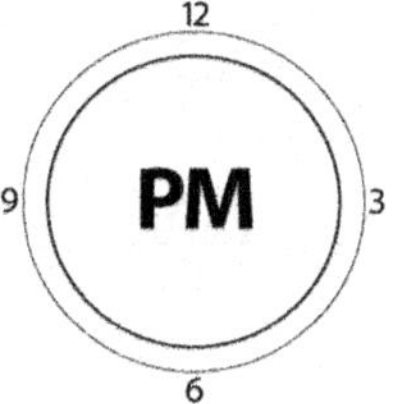
12
9
PM
3
6

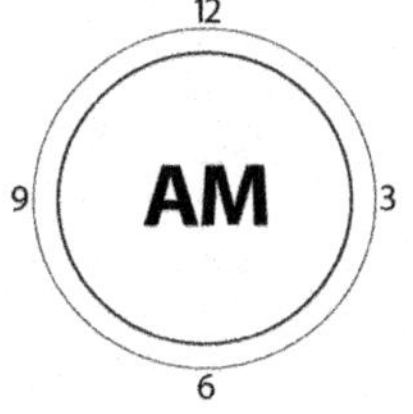
12
9
AM
3
6

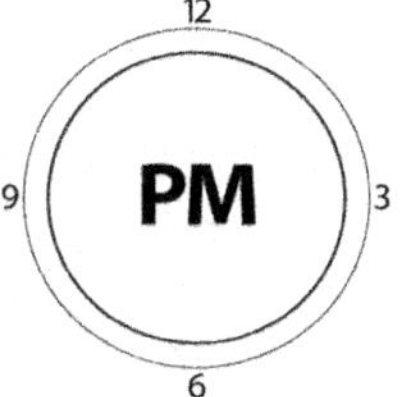
12
9
PM
3
6

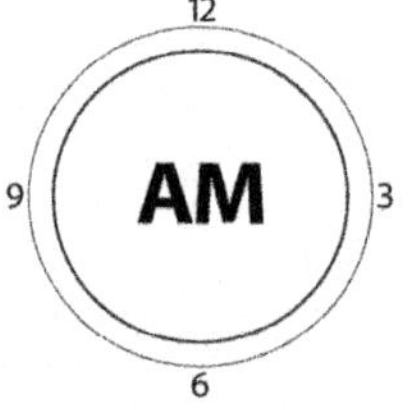
12
9
AM
3
6

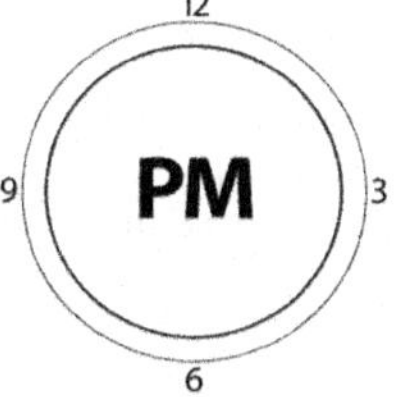
12
9
PM
3
6

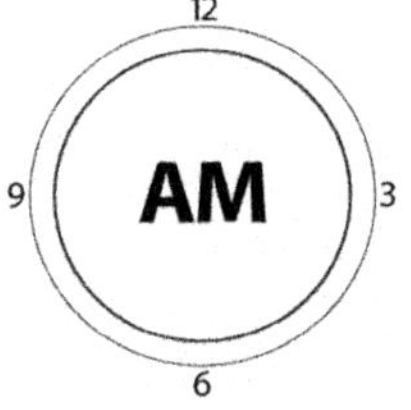
12
9
AM
3
6

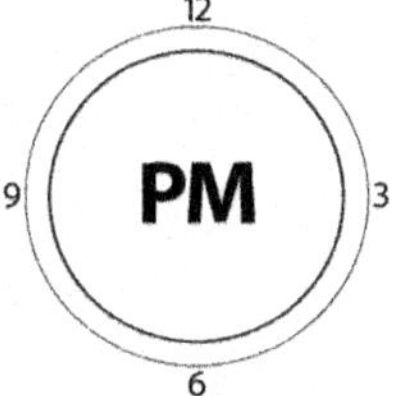
12
9
PM
3
6

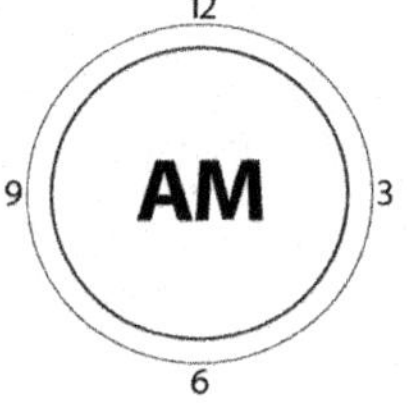
12
9
AM
3
6

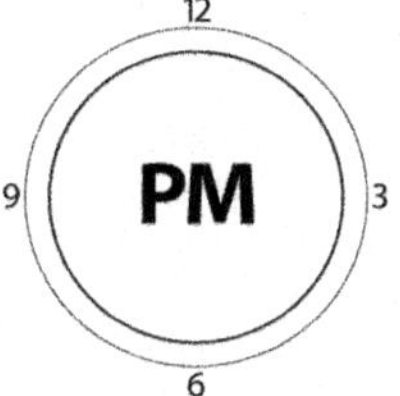
12
9
PM
3
6

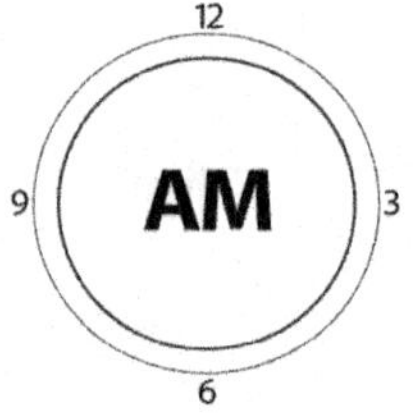
12
9
AM
3
6

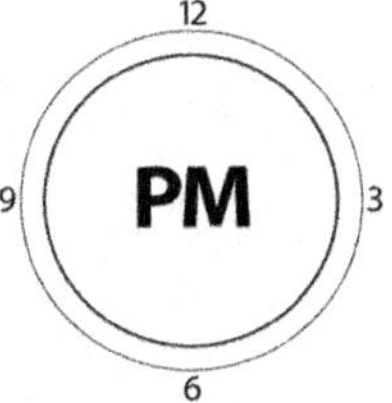
12
9
PM
3
6

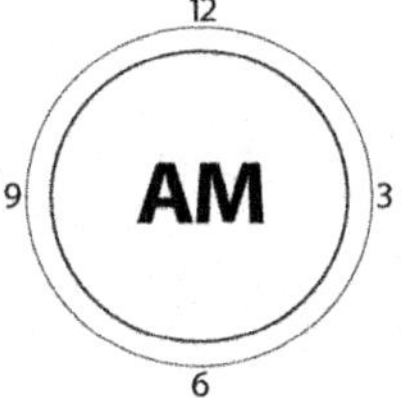
12
9
AM
3
6

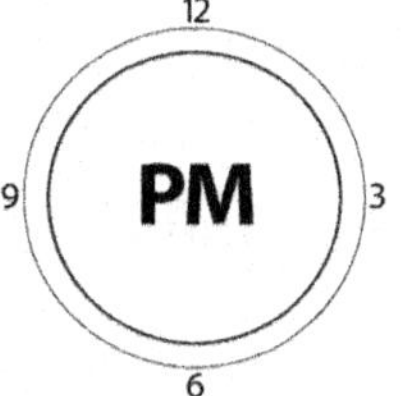
12
9
PM
3
6

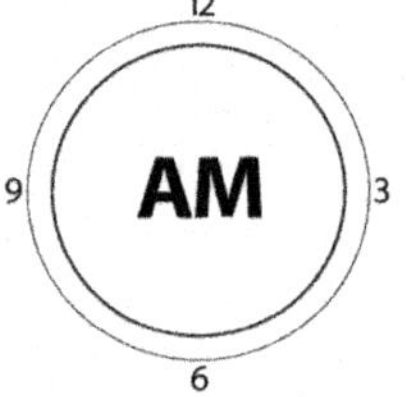
12
9
AM
3
6

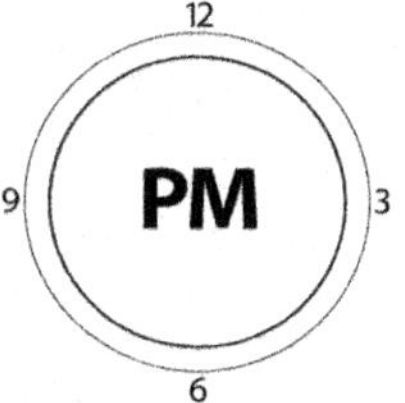
12
9
PM
3
6

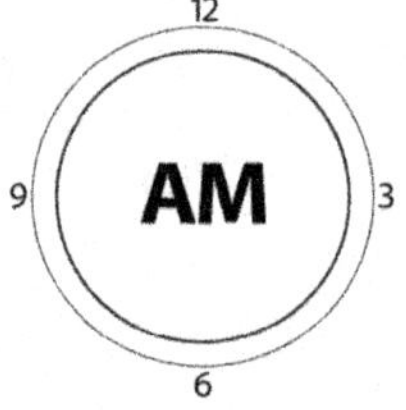
12
9
AM
3
6

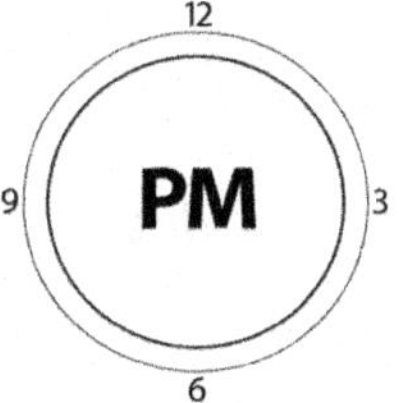
12
9
PM
3
6

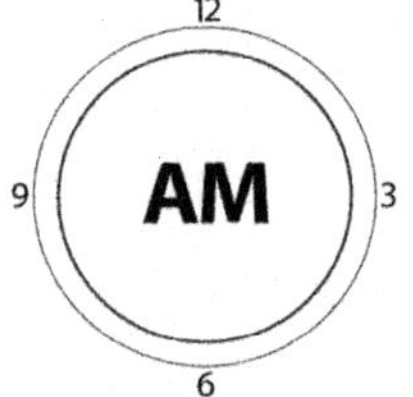
12
9
AM
3
6

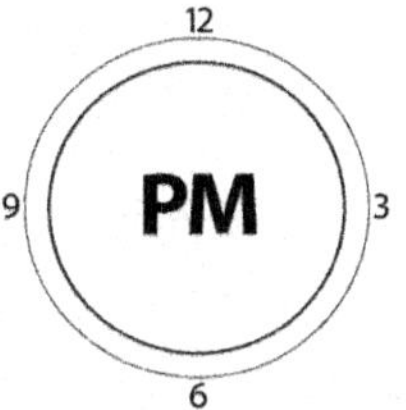
12
9
PM
3
6

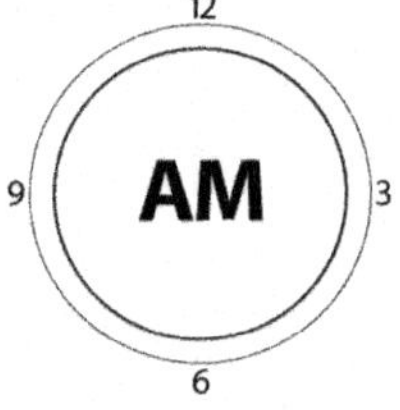
12
9
AM
3
6

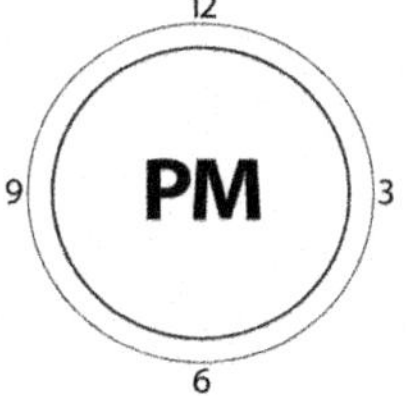
12
9
PM
3
6

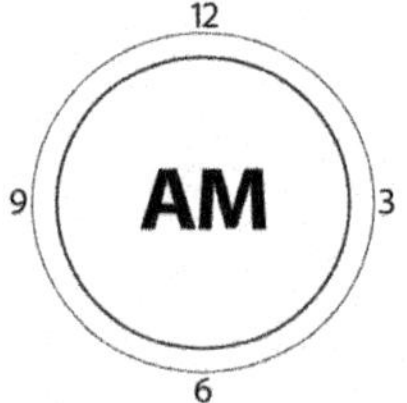
12
9
AM
3
6

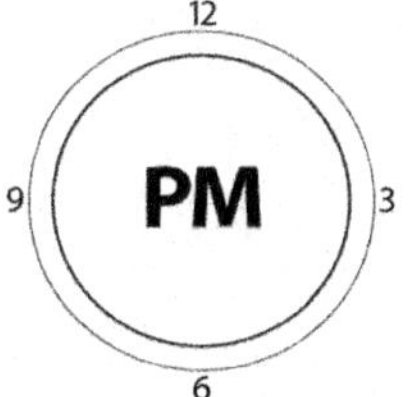
12
9
PM
3
6

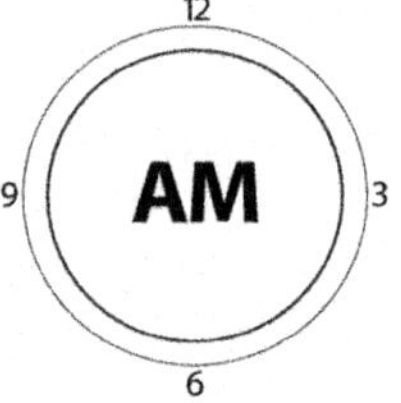
12
9
AM
3
6

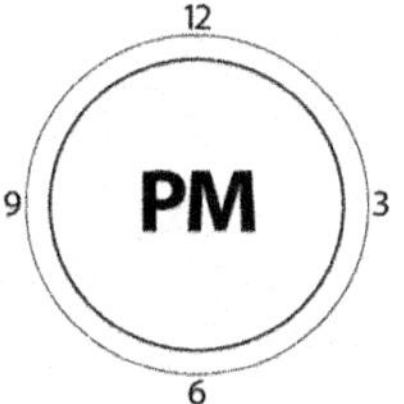
12
9
PM
3
6

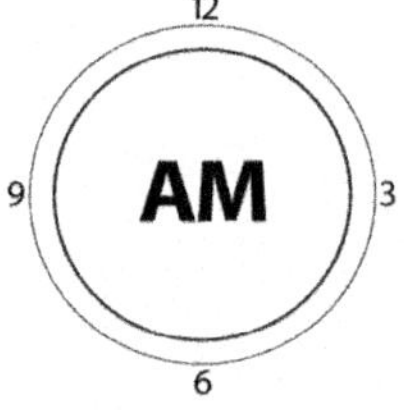
12
9
AM
3
6

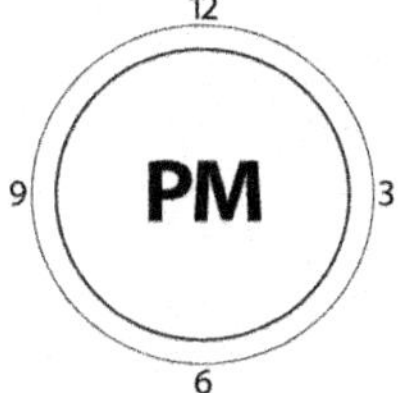
12
9
PM
3
6

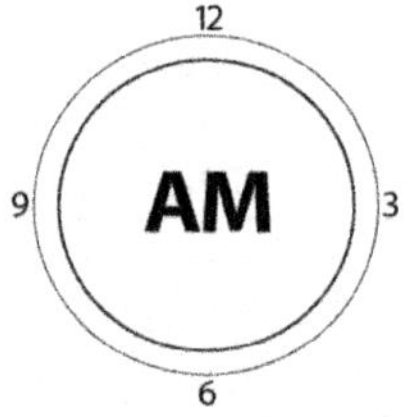
12
9
AM
3
6

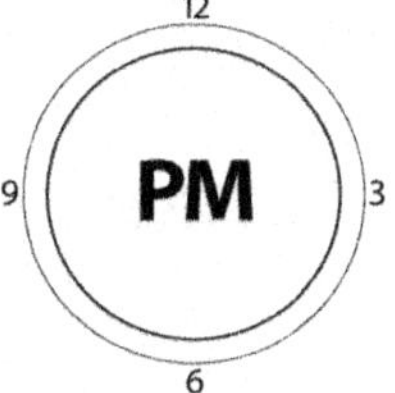
12
9
PM
3
6

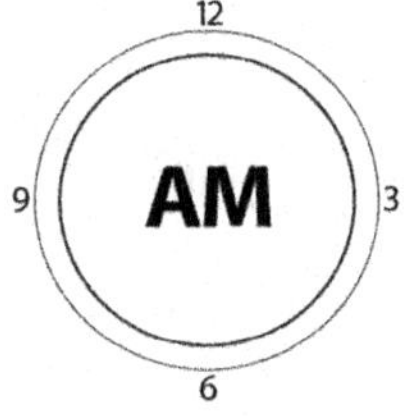
12
9
AM
3
6

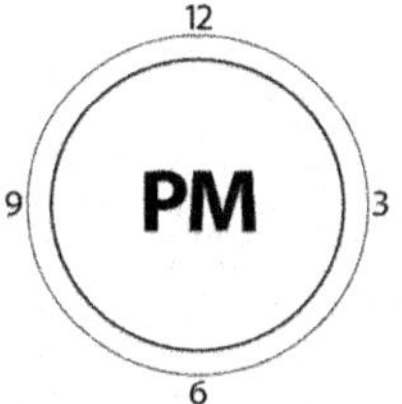
12
9
PM
3
6

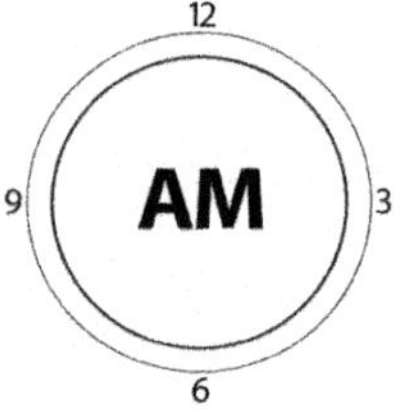
12
9
AM
3
6

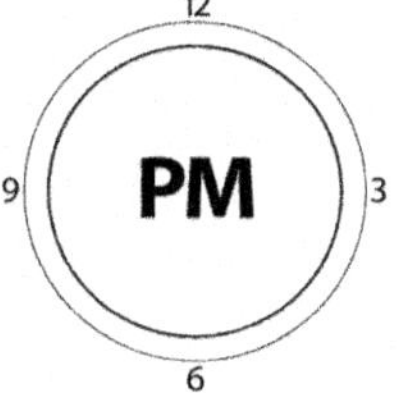
12
9
PM
3
6

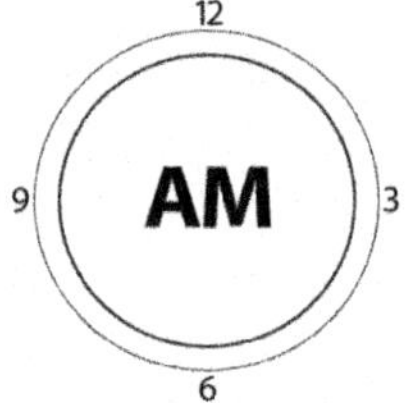
12
9
AM
3
6

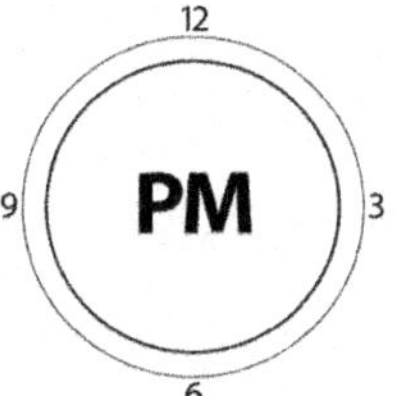
12
9
PM
3
6

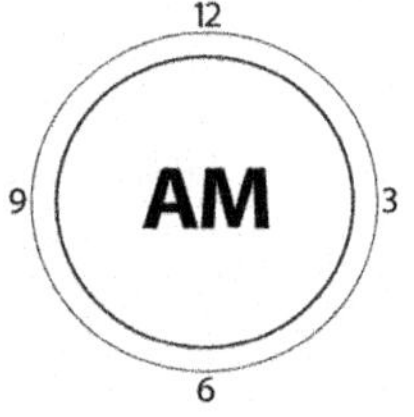
12
9
AM
3
6

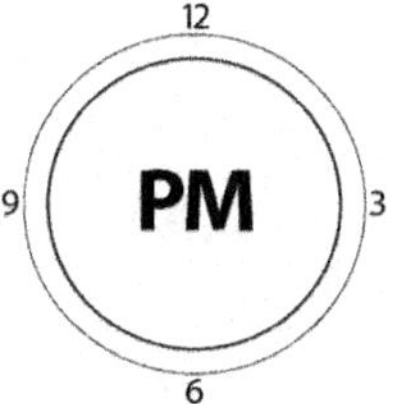
12
9
PM
3
6

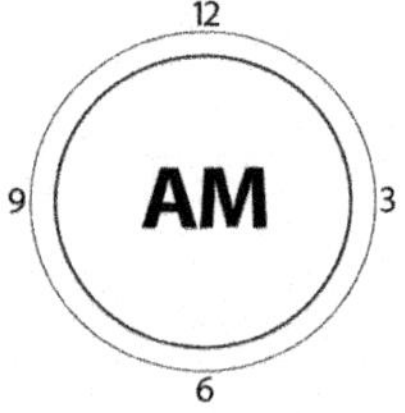
12
9
AM
3
6

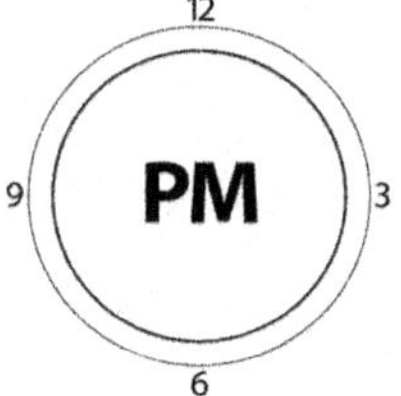
12
9
PM
3
6

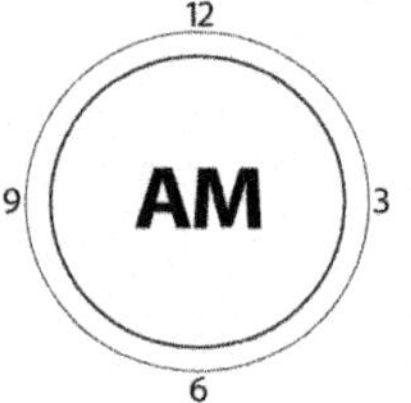
12
9
AM
3
6

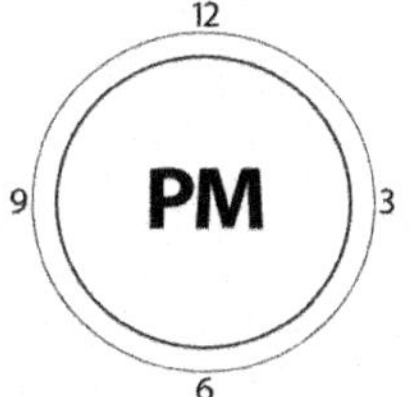
12
9
PM
3
6

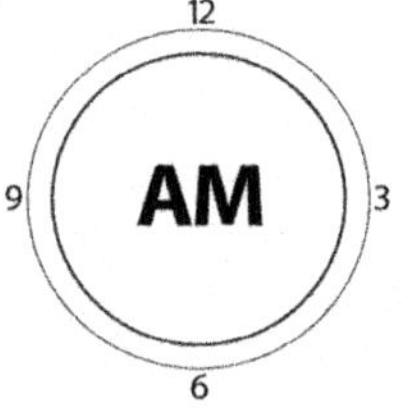
12
9
AM
3
6

12
9
PM
3
6

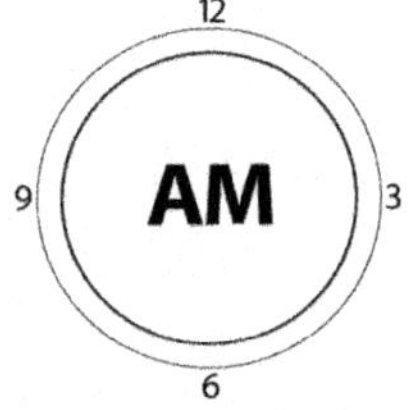
12
9
AM
3
6

12
9
PM
3
6

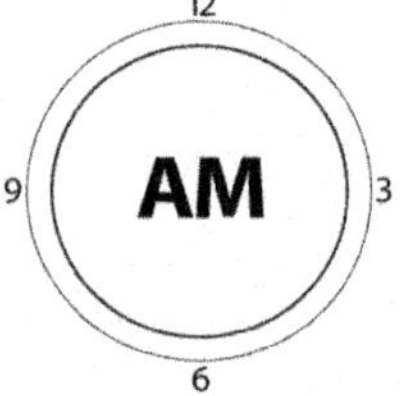
12
9
AM
3
6

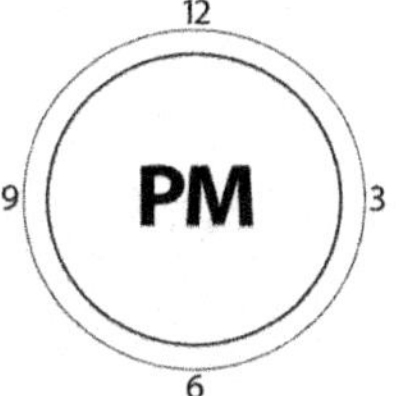
12
9
PM
3
6

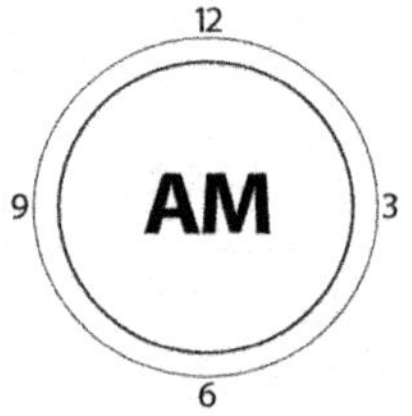
12
9
AM
3
6

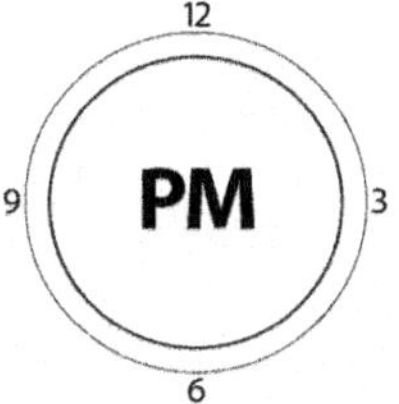
12
9
PM
3
6

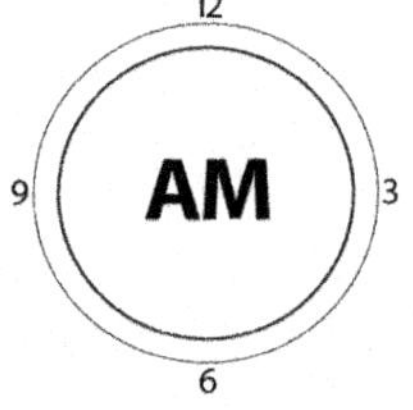
12
9
AM
3
6

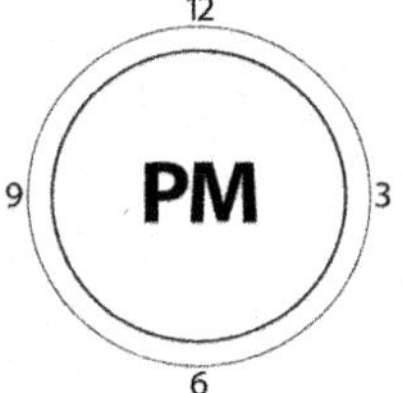
12
9
PM
3
6

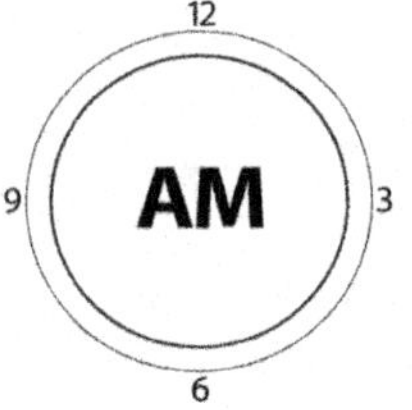
12
9
AM
3
6

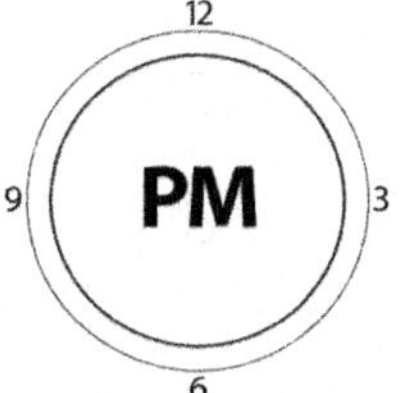
12
9
PM
3
6

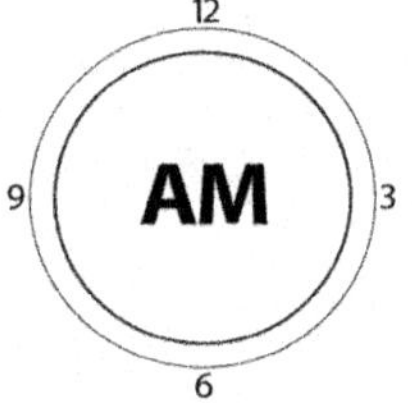
12
9
AM
3
6

12
9
PM
3
6

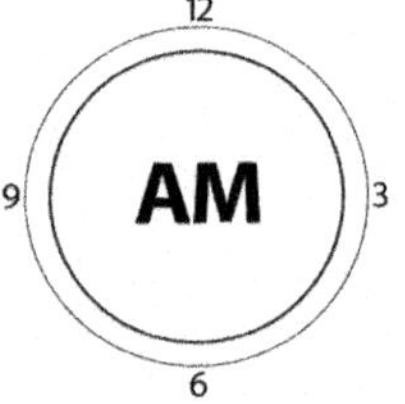
12
9
AM
3
6

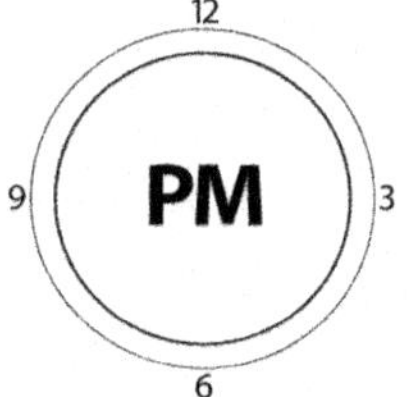
12
9
PM
3
6

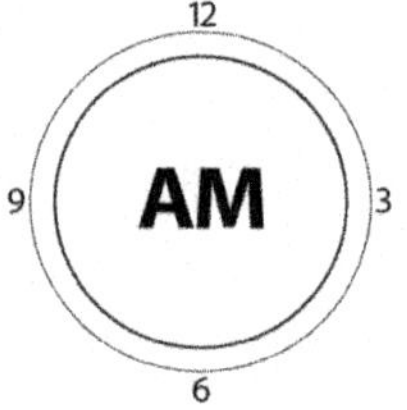
12
9
AM
3
6

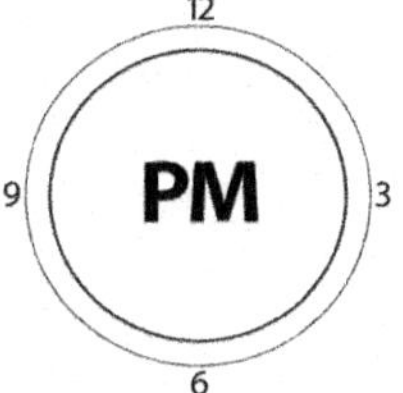
12
9
PM
3
6

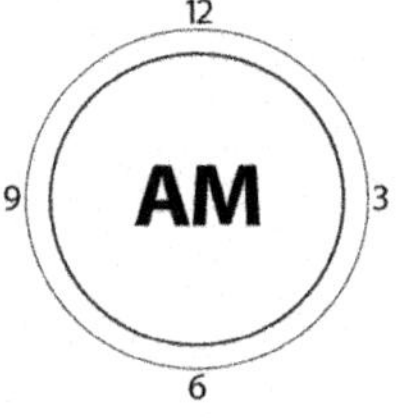
12
9
AM
3
6

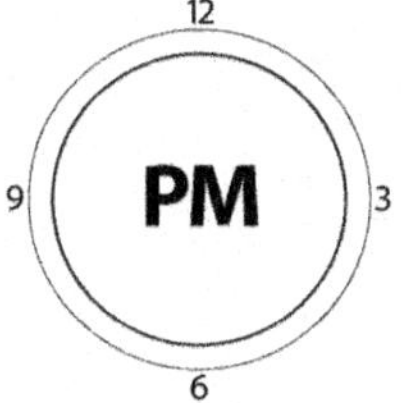
12
9
PM
3
6

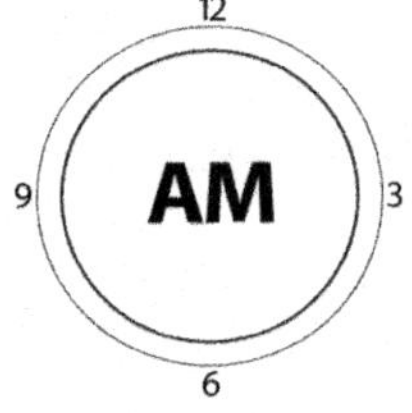
12
9
AM
3
6

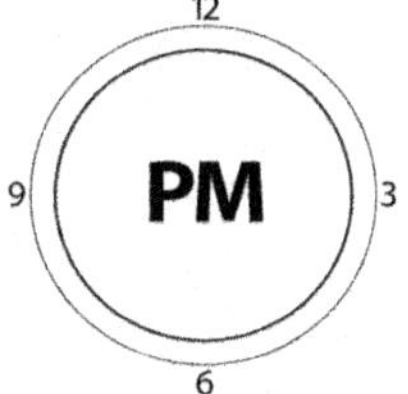
12
9
PM
3
6

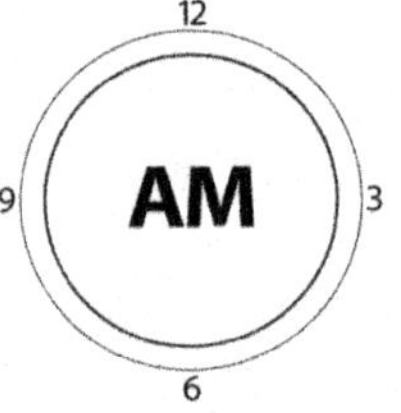
12
9
AM
3
6

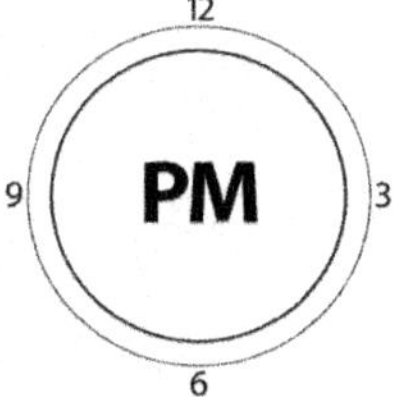
12
9
PM
3
6

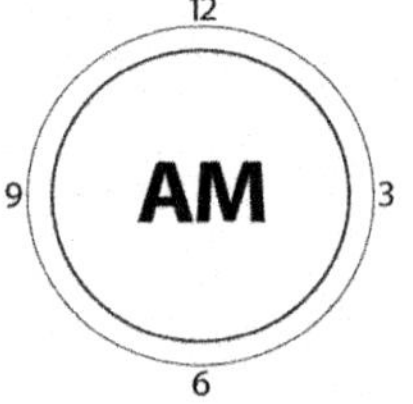
12
9
AM
3
6

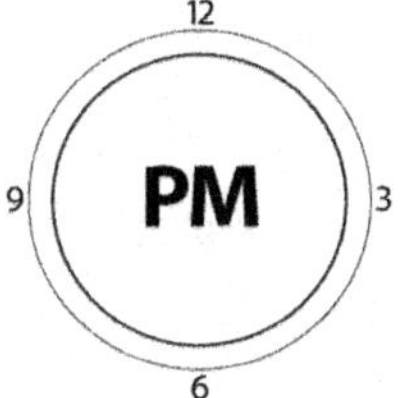
12
9
PM
3
6

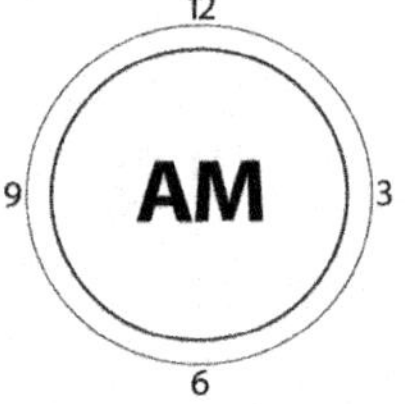
12
9
AM
3
6

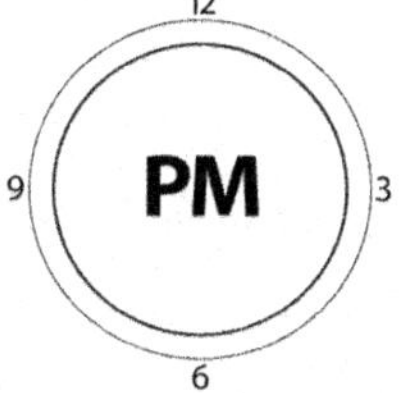
12
9
PM
3
6

Need a replacement?
Get your next planner at

ClockMapDailyPlanner.com

CPSIA information can be obtained at www.ICGtesting.com
Printed in the USA
LVOW04s1354070915

453138LV00022B/476/P